Staying Safe in a Wired World
A Parent's Guide to Internet Safety

Nickel Publishing

Staying Safe
in a
Wired World

A Parents' Guide to Internet Safety

© 2006 by Rob Nickel

Published by Nickel Publishing
(a division of Nickel Concepts)
250 Dundas St. South, Unit #6,
Cambridge, Ontario. N1R 8A8

Printed in Canada

Library and Archives Canada Cataloguing in Publication

Nickel, Rob, 1968-
Staying safe in a wired world : a parent's guide to internet safety / Rob Nickel.

Includes index.
ISBN 0-9780082-0-0

1. Internet and children. 2. Internet--Safety measures. I. Title.

HQ784.I58N53 2006   303.48'34'083   C2006-900453-6

Copy Editor - Barry Nayler

Cover and Book Design by Rob Nickel

For current information about all releases from Nickel
Publishing (*A Division of Nickel Concepts*) please visit our website.

www.nickelpublishing.com

Credits

Microsoft product screenshots reprinted with permission from Microsoft Corporation.

Screenshots reproduced with permission of Yahoo! Inc. © 2006 by Yahoo! Inc. YAHOO! and the YAHOO! Logo are trademarks of Yahoo! Inc.

Screenshots of ICQ and the Flower Logo are trademarks and/or registered trademarks of ICQ in the U.S. and/or other countries worldwide.

Definitions copyrighted by and reprinted with permission of WhatIs.com and TechTarget, Inc.

The AOL.com triangle logo is a trademark of America Online, Inc. AOL is a registered trademark of America Online, Inc. The AOL.com screenshot is (c) 2006 by America Online, Inc. America Online content, name, Running Man Icon, icons and trademarks are used with permission.

Statistical information and charts provided by The Media-Awareness Network with their permission.

Every effort was made to ensure that the how-to steps, websites, and links listed were accurate as of the date of publication. Such information may be subject to change without notice.

In Memory Of

In memory of my mother Joyce Nickel who was always proud of her children. The last words she spoke to me were "I love you and I am very proud of you." She would always tell me "Just keep doing what you're doing and it will all work out" and those words will stay with me forever.

Thanks Mom.

Dedication

To all of the men and women in law enforcement, who put their lives on the line every day to make sure that not only our children are safe but that we are all safe.

Contents

Chapter 4

Chapter 5

Chapter 6

About the Author

Rob Nickel is a leading expert on Internet Safety. He created and maintains www.cyber-safety.com and retired from the Ontario Provincial Police after a 14-year career.

In 1989 Rob joined the Ontario Provincial Police and worked at the Simcoe Detachment in uniform patrol until 1992. In 1992 Rob was promoted to Detective Constable and worked with the 3 District Criminal Investigations Unit conducting investigations such as major drug investigations, serious sexual assaults and homicide investigations.

In 1996 Rob transferred to the OPP Child Pornography Section as a Detective Constable where he started working undercover online, dealing with pedophiles who traded child pornography, and attempted to lure children for sex. During this time Rob lectured to many police officers on online undercover techniques, the workings of the Internet in relation to criminal offences and the identification of child pornography. Rob was also deemed an expert in these areas in the Superior Court of Ontario, and has testified in numerous trials dealing with Internet crimes. In 2000 Rob was promoted to Detective Sergeant (second in command) of the Child Pornography Section. He continued to lecture and conduct online undercover operations as well as organize major projects in Ontario as well as a Canada wide project involving 73 officers across Canada.

Rob is globally recognized as an expert in online undercover investigations, and has lectured in a number of countries throughout the world including France, Belgium, Spain and Brazil. He is a professional speaker who conducts presentations for parenting groups and educators on the dangers of the Internet. He is also an inspirational speaker who in 2004 was one of nine finalists for the World Championship of Public Speaking held in Reno, Nevada. To become one of nine finalists Rob had to win 5 levels of competition that began with over 30,000 contestants.

Rob is currently president of Nickel Concepts. Nickel Concepts is a multimedia company creating websites, producing interactive material including video production and editing. Nickel Concepts is also the Canadian distributor of RAZZUL software, through its Kid Innovation Canada Division of the company. RAZZUL is safe Internet browsing software for children 3 to 12 years old.

Rob is married and lives in Cambridge, Ontario with his wife Kim and 2 daughters Veda and Georgia.

Acknowledgments

I would first like to thank my wife Kim who has always believed in everything I have taken on in my life, and who has taken the time to push me to get this book completed. She is not only a beautiful person but also the best mother in the world. Our two beautiful daughters Veda and Georgia are evidence of this. My girls have given me inspiration to try and help protect other children in the world from online dangers, and have always been there to give me support in anything I try. They were patient with me on the days I could not go places with them because of my writing and speaking and for that I am truly thankful.

Thanks also to my father who taught me when I was younger to never settle for, but to see something through to the end no matter what obstacles are in the way.

Special thanks to the Ontario Provincial Police who gave me employment for 14 years in a job I loved, and who gave me the opportunity to travel the world speaking to other police officers on online undercover investigations. I would especially like to thank the members of the Child Pornography Section who I am still in contact with and who do a job not many officers would like to do. They are a special bunch of men and women who spend their days making the Internet safer for children. Officers are never really thanked enough for the work that they do, but this book is dedicated to all of those men and women who keep our streets safe, and our children protected by doing what they do.

Introduction

Policing the Dark Side of the Net

As a police officer I had seen a lot of things during my career that would make the average person cringe. I had dealt with many different individuals who not only had little respect for others but also had little respect for themselves. I conducted major drug investigations, sexual assaults and homicide investigations and I thought I had seen it all until I entered the world of online child pornography trading as an undercover officer.

In 1996 I transferred to the Child Pornography Section as a Detective Constable, working undercover by taking on the role of a pedophile. I spent my days talking and meeting with those who try and lure and harm our children on the Internet. The most shocking aspect for me in doing such a job was that the individuals I was dealing with were your every day Joe. They had occupations ranging from computer technician to doctors and journalist to CEO's of major corporations. These were not the stereotypical old men wearing trench coats hanging out at the playgrounds (although a lot of these individuals did hang out in such places). Most of these men were well-educated, intelligent hard-working family men. Some of course were very different, loners who stayed at home on their computers all day and had no 'real life' friends, but for the most part they were your average Joe, your next door neighbour.

One thing people have to realize is that pedophiles (those who's sexual interest are children) know how to bond with children easily. They make it a study, and know how to build a rapport with children; they know the "hot buttons" to build that bond. They also know that it is very easy to build that bond "site unseen", meaning without the influence of appearance (typing over the Internet) it is very easy to strike up a friendship and become 'pals' with children. When I would meet with them face to face for a drink (working undercover of course) I was always amazed at how they loved the Internet because of the opportunity to talk with so many children, and build that bond. The Internet became heaven on earth for pedophiles.

You can't do much to prepare yourself for such a job, that is for sure, but after 7 years of doing this work I gained a great understanding of what these predators look for, and how they hunt their prey on the Information Highway. It gave me the knowledge of not only what kids should do to keep safe online but WHY they should do those things. It is always easy to step back and say, "well you should not do this" and "never do that" but throughout this book I will be telling you why! I will give examples of past cases I have investigated and give you a better understanding of why these rules for children and parents are so important to follow. I now spend a lot of my time lecturing to parenting groups and educators on Internet Safety, and I am always amazed at how many parents and teachers approach me after the seminar and have a look of fear on their face of what I have just shown during the presentation. My motive in writing this book is not to scare, but to educate. Unfortunately we usually learn better when we have fear as a motivator. I wanted to write a book that was easy for any parent to read (without getting technical) and could be shared with their children as well. Most people ask me if I hate the Internet or think it is something that will ruin society, and I always state the exact opposite. I feel the Internet is a great place for learning and entertainment, but like anything else it has to be used properly, and those who use it must understand the risks.

I am usually swamped by e-mails after presentations explaining how as parents they are getting involved in their children's online activity, and really had no idea in the past what their children were up to online. They explain that because of my seminar or speech they now have their children protected, so I knew I had to do something to reach the masses, and decided to take everyone's suggestion and write this book.

This book is about protecting our children and ourselves from the dangers that lurk online. To give parents and their children the knowledge of the uses of the Internet and how to get the most out of it while staying safe. Happy Surfing – and be safe!

Chapter One

What is the Internet?

"There are no seven wonders of the world in the eyes of a child. There are seven million."

Walt Streightiff

Chapter 1

What is the Internet?

Think of the Internet as a huge city with many different places to visit. There are all sorts of educational places, places for entertainment, and some places to get into trouble. When you say the Internet to some people they think of chat rooms, others think for web pages or surfing the net, and others will think of e-mail. These are all parts of the Internet and I will expand on them in this book, but the truth is, all of these things are part of the Internet which is now part of all our lives. There are not too many people who have not used one part of the Internet in some way. There are some parts of this huge city that are dangerous for children and adults, and the only way to avoid these places is to be educated on their existence.

The Internet is a worldwide network of computers hooked together through different means (coax, fiber cable, telephone lines, satellite, wireless transmissions) that let 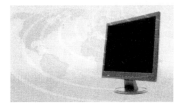 everyone have access to the rest, and the information contained on them. It is not owned by anyone or really monitored or controlled by any agency although many police agencies throughout the world are now doing their best to monitor the illegal activity that occurs on the Internet.

Think of a huge spider web of computers hooked together to create the sharing of information throughout the world. No matter where you are on this web, you can get to any other place by following the threads of silk web. In fact I designed a logo of the Ontario Provincial Police Child Pornography Section (also known as Project "P") and it was a spider web with a "P" in the middle of it. It was well received because it explained exactly what we did.

Technically the Internet dates back to 1969 when it was called ARPANET (Advanced Research Projects Agency Network). The U.S. Department of Defense created a decentralized network of computers that would stay connected in the event of a nuclear strike during the Cold War by being "self-healing". In other words if one part of the network was destroyed or damaged it would find another route to it's location (if one part of that spider web had a hole in it – it would just go around another route). In later years other networks were connected to ARPANET until it became "The Internet".

By 1984 the number of Internet hosts broke the "over 1000" mark and in 1989 the Internet Relay Chat (IRC) was developed by Jarkko Oikarinen. The IRC is where I did a lot of the undercover trading in child pornography and this will be explained later in this book, but basically it is numerous chat channels where people can chat and trade files. In 1991 the World Wide Web (the Web or WWW) was invented by Tim Berners-Lee and Robert Cailau, and in 1993 the first web browser (Mosaic) was created by Marc Andreessen so people could view web pages. I got connected to the Internet in 1993 and have been online ever since.

The World Wide Web refers to all of the publicly available websites. This is just a part of the Internet, yet it is the one we hear most about because of websites advertised or that we search through for  information. It is used the most as well, and I have to be honest, I don't even use the yellow pages anymore, because if I need a phone number or any information I know it is at my fingertips on the Web.

Nobody owns the Internet, or manages it in any way. There is no company or government that can regulate it although I'm sure the debate will continue for years on regulating it .

I would normally say to have access to the Internet you would need your own ISP (Internet Service Provider) like AOL, Sympatico, or CompuServe, but with the day of wireless technology you could really drive into any neighbourhood and use a wireless connection from someone's house. Most homes with wireless Internet will have this connection secured, but you would be surprised at how many homes just keep this connection open and anyone within range can use their Internet connection to surf the net, or even do something illegal with it, including hacking into that homes' computer (*this will be covered in Chapter 3 of this book*).

To connect to the Internet you usually need an account with an Internet Service Provider. You pay them a fee to give you access to the Internet and you can gain this access in many different ways. Dialup access using a computer modem and a telephone line or high-speed access, which can be done through Cable Modem, DSL, Satellite or line of site wireless technology.

When you post something on the Internet it is there immediately for anyone to view; anyone in the world. One of the coolest things about the Internet is access to people around the world, as well as content from around the world. You can have knowledge with the click of a button. With the stroke of a key you can find answers to questions, pictures of your favorite star, or where to purchase that book you have been looking for. Technology has made research and information you need accessible, but it has also made it easy for criminals to do their work as well.

There are many different parts to the Internet and although the Internet uses the same network of computers to send information, sometimes they just do it in different ways. All information on the Internet is sent in small units called "packets" (electronic information that goes from one destination to another). We could go into detail about the technical aspects but this book was written for the average parent who just wants to know the dangers and the reasons why the safety rules should be followed. As an exercise, if you want to find out more about how the Internet really works (all the fun technical stuff) go on the net yourself and look it up; there are many different sites that will walk you through everything you need to know. I am going to cover some of the ways information and applications are used on the Internet, but I am going to keep it simple.

Criminals on the Net

The Good – The Bad – The Dangerous

In 1993 when I started to use the Internet, I was totally captivated by the information I had access to. I could search for things I would normally have to go to the library to find. I could talk to people  from around the world, and all it took was a long distance carrier (because there was no local Internet Service Provider in Simcoe, Ontario) and an Internet Service provider account in London (an hour drive away from Simcoe). After all that I was getting connection speeds up to a whopping 8kbps (today's dial-up connections are 58kbps and with my line of site wireless connection now I am getting 1300kbps – that is 162 times faster than 1993). At that time I was a police officer but never gave much thought to the idea that criminal offences would take place over the Internet. I don't think anyone really knew just how big and powerful this "Internet" thing was going to be. People were still looking for the 'anykey' on computers so they could get them started.

My father started a computer software company in 1974 so I grew up around computers and knew a little about them, but they were all mainframe computers using terminals. Most people in 1993 were getting home computers but they were still like the VCR's of the 1980's where people still could not set the clock on them. I was one of the very few in our OPP detachment that did search warrants using computers, and had an old laptop computer I borrowed from my fathers' company to do work on. If someone told me that we would be walking around today with laptops getting wireless connections almost anywhere we go (even as I sit here in my local library typing this book and receiving e-mail) I would have said you are crazy, yet here we are in a wired world.

In 1996 when I joined the OPP Child Pornography Section, I had 3 years experience on the Internet and knew this was the new tool for criminals, and no officers had really taken on the role of doing online undercover work. Child pornography trading before the Internet was a very secretive and almost undetectable crime because before the digital age, photography-developing studios were needed and storage for the product had to be large because of the printed material. The other factor that was the most important is that the Internet and computers gave the Child Pornography Trading community a medium for trafficking. Now, groups were formed for like-minded people whose sexual interests were children. Other than a few different organizations such as N.A.M.B.L.A. (North American Man Boy Love Association), there was no way for these individuals to communicate. Now with the Internet and chat rooms, they could not only communicate, but distribute and store child pornography easily and with little risk of getting caught.

The Ontario Provincial Police knew this was coming and expanded their Child Pornography Section in 1996 and it was a great move. We got on the Internet wave quickly and learned how the child pornographers did business. My first case with the section turned out to be the largest seizure of Child Pornography in North America. With over 100,000 images and movies of Child Pornography on one individual's computer (which today is a typical seizure, if not considered very small), it made a lot of news coverage, and the government and the public took notice that the Internet did indeed have a dark side.

During that investigation I learned a lot about how these individuals do business over the Internet, and although most people still believe Child Pornography distribution is a money- maker, most of the distribution is done on trade, meaning collections are built by trading file for file. Child Pornography collectors like to expand their collections by trading.

Although they trade files, I soon found out they also trade secrets on how to groom and lure children as well. I started becoming friends with many of the individuals I interacted with on the Internet. They taught me their culture (thinking I was a pedophile as well) and how to become a better collector, and abuser. I soon found out just how serious they take their 'hobby', how they prey on the children who are loners, on the computer all the time, who have little or no parental supervision. They study children's likes and dislikes by reading teen and preteen magazines. What is cool and what isn't cool, what the latest big thing is. On one investigation I had a young female uniform officers pose as my 8-year-old daughter over the phone to a suspect in Newfoundland. He wanted to speak with me and my daughter, so before the call I gave this officer some study material. I then quizzed her on the Spice Girls (they were big in 1996 and 1997) and when the time came for the phone call and I handed the phone over to my supposed daughter, his first question to her was, "who is your favorite Spice Girl?", and she responded "Sporty Spice". They keep track of the latest kid craze; they do their homework, so as parents we have to do ours to keep our children safe.

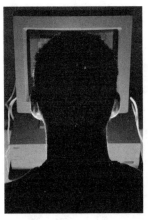

The predators on the Internet are only one type of online criminal. Others on the Internet enjoy hacking into computers to destroy your personal files, or gain access to your bank codes and passwords so they can transfer funds or use your account to pay for their purchases.

The Internet is also the new playground for bullies. Bullies use to be the big kids at school who stole your lunch money, but not anymore. Cyber-Bullies are now catching the wave, and surfing the net to find those to intimidate. With the new day and age of online chat programs and personal websites, bullies are having a hay day with intimidating other kids and making life miserable for some. This includes having someone access your computer and accessing your webcam and microphone on your computer to invade your privacy.

In the wired world everything is at your fingertips – including inappropriate sites for children. Pornography and hate sites pop up all over the place. You can access pornography sites without having to verify your age in any way. You can search out pornography and view images that should not be viewed by children.

There are also sites dedicated to showing people how to create illegal things such as bombs which can be very dangerous for children to view. I know of an individual who had a son who tried to create a bomb from instructions on the Internet and now has only 2 fingers left on one hand. Knowledge is power, but too much power in a child's hand can be very dangerous.

Sites showing people how to get a "high" off of household material is also a concern I have. These substances can be very dangerous and there are news stories every day of children dying from misuse of cleaning products.

Don't let the Internet scare you just because you don't know exactly how it works; after all I have no idea how a car engine works. I failed Auto Shop in high school, I am not mechanically inclined whatsoever, but I still buckle my children up when they are riding in the car. We have to make sure our kids are buckled up on the information highway just like on the regular highway. This book will give you the tools you need to help your children stay safe in a wired world.

Chapter Two

Benefits of the Net

"Parents can only give good advice or put them on the right paths, but the final forming of a person's character lies in their own hands."

Anne Frank

Chapter 2

Benefits of the Internet

Well this subject could be a book in itself. Many people think I dislike the Internet because of the dangers found within it, but that could not be further from the truth. In fact, I believe the Internet is one of the most important technological tools in this day and age. The Internet makes it possible to do so many different things, which in turn makes our lives easier, and a little more interesting. I could not imagine a world without it, what would we spend our time doing? Where would we find information? Where would we find a plumber to fix our toilets? Where would we find out who JLo is dating, or marrying for that matter?

This vehicle of information and communication is valuable; it helps in all aspects or our life. It is as important as the vehicles we drive, but remember we wear seatbelts and have to wear them on the information highway as well.

Education

The Internet has made education more accessible for a lot of people. For those who cannot attend schools because of transportation problems, physical inabilities, or because they have different schedules that make it impossible to attend classes there is now hope. Universities and Colleges offer online courses so you can work towards your degree, or take that course you have always wanted to take. They

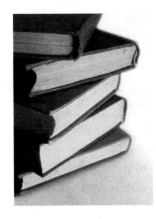

offer courses online that will help your advancement in your work, or your personal life. Study material, tests, and assignments are sent back and forth via e-mail, or stored on the Institutions website for the students to download. You can also communicate with other students on message boards, or live chats to discuss the class and the topics. Test scores are usually given at the completion of the test because they are done online, and the instructors are usually a click away with a simple e-mail. I have taken a University course online and I have to admit it was tough, but very interesting and economical. I have a pretty busy schedule with running a couple of different companies, and speaking all over the world, and with these types of courses I can do assignments and tests from hotel rooms, Internet cafes or even on vacation with my family.

Our children use the Internet for doing research on their in-class assignments. I remember as a child using National Geographic and the Encyclopedia as my resources for all assignments. Now our children have a massive amount of material to choose from on the Internet. There are websites dedicated to helping in the education of children through research. There are also websites that are dedicated to helping children learn reading, writing and math with interactive online games. My two daughters have used these sites and my wife and I have noticed improvement in their grades as a result. It makes learning fun, while at the same time it helps them build confidence in their ability to do the work.

The Internet is also a great resource for teachers to keep up to date with the latest learning techniques, testing and new websites designed to help children increase their learning while having fun. Reading skills are improved by the Internet, providing interesting material for children to read. Children can search out sites of their interest and read up on them which is the key to getting your child to read more.

RAZZUL software by Kid Innovation is by far the best Internet safe browsing software out there for children. It is the reason my company got involved with them. The reason I am such a supporter of this software (found at www.kidinnovation.ca) is because it is filled with not only entertaining child approved sites, but packed full of the educational sites as well. It was built with the parent in mind.

There are options to send messages to your children from work (i.e. "good job on your test today Johnny") as well as total control on who they send e-mail to and receive e-mail from. Parents can also monitor sites they are visiting and block access to sites that may not be approved by Kid Innovation (i.e. a site they need to access for researching a school project only needs a password by the parent so they can view it). It is a great environment for learning and parents also appreciate the fact that the computer is locked down as well so children cannot delete files or change programs. The only software the children are allowed to access on the computer are those programs the parents allow. This was a huge plus for me as I knew first hand how children can accidentally erase or change files on the computer by clicking here and there. I touch on Internet filtering and blocking in Chapter 10, but this is my book and I want to recommend the best. I have tested most of the programs out there and I choose RAZZUL! It has a 3-month trial included in the CD attached to this book so you test it out and let me know what your thoughts are; you will not be disappointed!

Communication

When I was a child I used the phone a lot. I lived out in the country so all my friends lived far away and the only way to communicate was to use the phone. Now we have a new way of communicating with our friends. It is by chatting online, and not only that but you can talk to other people around the world and learn different cultures, or have pen pals from places you have never heard of. E-mail has changed the way the world communicates. I actually can't remember the last time I sent a letter to someone. I have all my friends and family's e-mail addresses, so I send letters that way. Just recently I sent an e-mail to my cousin in Las Vegas to tell her and her husband that my wife and I were coming down for a few days away. I know I could have called, but then I would have to pay long distance (man am I cheap) and they would have had to write down the dates and times. By using e-mail, they have a record right there that they can print out and use as a reminder. There is no postage to pay and you can even send pictures, or attach a birthday or anniversary wish card in the e-mail. The Internet is all about communication. New voice over

IP (Internet Protocol) is one of the newest breakthroughs that has really impressed me. I use a certain program on my computer that can dial telephone numbers and the call is just as clear, if not clearer, than a regular phone. As a matter of fact if I use the Voice Over IP software with another Internet user, it is like the person is sitting right beside me. It is amazing stuff, and it only gets better as technology improves.

My company, Nickel Concepts, has a number of different programmers all over the world because we have different divisions dealing with computer software, therefore, I am in constant communication with a number of different people all the time. I have all of these programmers and associates on different chat programs so I can just send them an instant message to get answers from them. I also use the voice over IP software to chat with them voice to voice and in some instances create a virtual meeting room where we have audio and video to communicate and can share applications like Microsoft word documents, PowerPoint slides, white boards, presentations, and any other type of program you can think of.

At the present time I am looking at setting up webinars (seminars conducted over the web) for public speaking, customer service and of course Internet Safety. This allows people to connect to a website where they will see me live, hear my voice, and see my presentation slides as well on the screen. I can answer questions  live with text chatting capabilities and conduct a presentation without the expense of a hotel conference room; and I can have this event open to not just my community, but the world! When I hear the word communication my first thought is "the Internet". The possibilities are endless with the Internet and communication.

If you are interested in participating in any webinars I am holding please contact me at **rob@nickelconcepts.com** and I will send you a link of the webinars topics along with the time and dates of the events.

Entertainment

Enough about learning and education, what about having fun? The Internet is full of that. There are so many sites that are there for our personal enjoyment. Game sites for those of us who like to play some cards, or solve crosswords. Sites where we can catch up on our favourite sports as well as video games played against other players from across the globe. You can also see your favourite sporting events live on the Internet with live feeds to sporting portal sites, including horse racing, team sports and live up to the minute scores of your favourite teams.

I love to play Texas Hold'em and for my coffee breaks I play 15 minutes of cards online against others from around the world (but not for real money although you are able to deposit money into an actual account and play that way). It helps me get better at the game so maybe one day I can be a world poker champion (maybe 30 more years) and it also gives me enjoyment. I don't have to find a local poker game to go to once a week; I can just log on to the website and play others with play money. I can also use the Internet to find out about other entertainment such as what movie is playing at my local theater. I never go to the newspaper anymore to see what is playing; I just go to a website dedicated to listing all the movies in my local theaters. It is easy to search but it gets even better because I can actually click on the trailer for the movie and see the preview to make sure it is the one I want to see. The Internet is an entertainment playground with all types of activities that will suit anyone.

Current Events

When breaking news happens the best place to go is the Internet. I remember when the terrorist attacks happened on 9/11 I was in my office in Toronto at the Child  Pornography Section. I happened to be on a news site on the Internet and read something about a plane hitting a building in New York. We turned on the TV to see if the news was covering it, and as we did we saw the second plane hit the second tower. It was on the Internet fast and after the incident we could go onto the CNN site and find the footage of it all, just moments after it happened. News feeds use the Internet to distribute their stories. If you want to find out about a news incident you can either watch TV and wait to see if they cover the story or go online and just type in what you are looking for and find the story in print or video in a matter of seconds.

Internet search sites can search all dedicated news and information sites for up-to-the-minute news. You can also subscribe to some of these sites to be notified if certain type of news happens. I like to keep up-to-date on the latest safety software for the Internet and the new dangers that are lurking online so the Internet has helped me. I have the Google News search notify me whenever an article is in a publication or on the net with certain keywords in it like "Internet Danger" or "Police Internet" and others. I also have it notify me if the name Rob Nickel appears, because I speak to so many different news agencies, I like to keep copies for myself and it gets hard to keep track, but the Google news sends me a link when it sees my name. Talk about time saving!

Hobbies or Interests

If you have certain hobbies or interests then the Internet is the place for you to keep in touch with others. You can find out the scoop on your favourite sports teams or if you are interested in cars or cooking there are groups or networks of people with the same interests who talk on message boards or newsgroups.

 The Internet is a network, and it can be a network for like-minded people who share their interests or hobbies. If you are into cooking you can find sites devoted to sharing recipes for Thanksgiving, or other holidays, or just

share recipes in general. If you have been diagnosed with cancer, there are groups devoted to helping you through a tough time, by chatting with others who have gone through that as well.

When my mother was diagnosed with cancer, my father spent hours on the computer doing research and reading what others had done to combat the dreaded disease. Like I said earlier, I love the Internet for the information we can gather to help our lives. These are just a few of the things you can find. It does not matter how small your hobby or interest, I am sure there is a site dedicated to it or a newsgroup that discusses the topic.

The Internet is also used to try and find long lost school friends or acquaintances through alumni sites, or just doing a search for your friends name to see if they were in the news or have a web site. Every now and again I go to an alumni site to see who has registered or to see what others I went to high school and college with are up to now. Many have put information in a profile and just the other week I found one of my friends and e-mailed him to see how he was doing. It was interesting to find out that he now publishes different magazines and has his own business as well. We then connected and had breakfast to catch up. This would not have been possible without the Internet unless I bumped into him on the street, which would have been almost impossible since he lives in a city an hour away.

Online Shopping

Although my wife is the shopping expert in our home, I am the online shopping expert, that is for sure. There are

dangers with purchasing things online but I have had nothing but positive experiences, probably due to being extra careful. I only order products online if the site is a reputable one, such as Amazon (for most of my book needs) or Indigo/Chapters online. I still like browsing in the bookstore but I have found I can get a better price ordering online and having the books shipped. I can even order second-hand books at a fraction of the price. One book I actually paid 1 penny for – the best deal yet, and it was second-hand from a library and there is not a mark on it, only the library code on the spine of the book. I used to spend hundreds of dollars a year on new books; now I have cut my spending greatly and they usually arrive in less than a week!

Most of the major retailers in the world are online, and the sites are easy to use and are extremely useful to busy people who find it hard to get out to the stores at Christmas or other gift-giving occasions. I am actually writing this section at Christmas time and I am just waiting for some of my orders to arrive. I did my shopping in the comfort of my own home.

You can buy anything on the Internet and I have purchased many different items over the years. It is easy to find the deals if you know where to look. I have used EBay to purchase a video camera, and I often look on EBay for electronic equipment for my company. If you have the time and want to save some money, online shopping is not a bad deal. You must, however, make sure the site is reputable and that the information you give them to make the purchase is secure. You will be able to buy this book online when it is complete from my site and others, and it will be good for me as a businessperson due to the amount of people I can reach on the Internet. I am hoping to sell this book not only in Canada but throughout the world, and with the Internet that is very possible.

Travel

The Internet is global so you can boldly go where others have gone before. You can see the world on the Internet because the whole world is connected. How exciting when your children can virtually visit other countries just by browsing the Net! Children can practice their communication skills, learn different cultures and experience other languages just by traveling online. Families can learn about the world together using technology as the vehicle to get them from place to place. We can visit these places in cyberspace, or we can use the Internet to arrange the actual travel.

I speak all over the world and usually make my own travel arrangements. I never use a travel agent because I can find the best deals (most of the time) and book everything myself online.  There are many travel sites out there that I use; it just depends on who has the best price on that flight. It is not just the flights you can book, but your hotel, car rental and entertainment tickets. Most of the travel sites are easy to navigate. You just fill out the time and date you want to leave and your destination and home location or airport and let their site do all the work for you. Some people still like to use travel agents which I have no problems with, but I found once you get used to booking online, it is fast and there are really no hassles (knock on wood).

The other exceptional part of using the Internet to book travel is the site you book with will have links to the resort you are staying at, you can pick your seats on the plane online, and they will even have links to events in the area that may interest you. This saves doing more searching for the hotel's site, or contacting the Chamber of Commerce to find out information. My wife and I love Las Vegas (I know what you are thinking – Texas Hold'em and Vegas - this guy has a problem!) so if we want to go down, I do a search for the cheapest airfare and accommodations and we pick where we stay from there. Our last trip to Las Vegas was a few months ago and we stayed at an excellent hotel for just $39.00/night (most hotels are $200.00 to $350.00/night) and our airfare was less than half the regular fare because I took 30 minutes to search out the best deal. We had a great stay and saved a ton of money – which is always a good thing!

Chapter Three

The Risks

"Children are our most valuable natural resource."

Herbert Clark Hoover

Chapter 3

The Risks

Well, we talked about the good the Internet has to share, now let's talk about the bad. This really is what this book was meant to show, the risks and dangers of the Internet. I love the Internet but have seen the dangers that lurk within it, and as parents we cannot turn a blind eye to the dangers. Education on what the risks are is important so we can take the steps needed to protect our children.

We all know that with the good stuff there is always some bad that comes with it. So let's talk about some of the not so good things, or risks that are out there in cyberspace that can potentially harm our children, and ourselves for that matter!

Predators

Of course this is my specialty, and my main purpose for writing this book. The Internet has created a great place for those people who want to harm our children. It has not only given them a vehicle to communicate with our children, but has also given them a perfect vehicle to communicate with each other. Just as prisoners in jail teach each other how to become better criminals, stalkers on the Internet teach each other how to become better child predators. They will hang out in child chat channels, answer message board postings from children and most dangerous of all, build a rapport with our children and gain their trust. Now don't start pulling the phone line out of the wall just yet. Out of the millions, perhaps billions of people online today, the predator is a very small minority, but they are there, and we have to be aware of this fact.

Pedophiles in particular are very good at what they do. They study, and develop their craft. That sounds pretty bad but it is true. They are great at building that rapport with kids, and know how to "type" with them and gain their trust. While meeting with many of these individuals I found out very fast that they love the chase, how to access children fast, and build that trust even faster. They realize that the more you know about your victim the better odds you have to get them to meet with you. This is why the personal information your children put on a website or a profile page is very critical. You are going to hear them say, "But mom, so-and-so has their information and picture up on their profile page!" My answer is of course, "Well you're not so-and-so!" I see this getting out of control as time goes on. It is so easy for me (and the bad guys) to get online, and gather information on a child in any city in the world. I do this in presentations, and now it is getting easier. Predators have a mass of information they can gather on their targets, and believe me there are many children in this world with a big bull's eye on them.

Children want to be accepted and understood. They want to belong and the predators make sure they feel this way online. They show affection to their targets, listen to their problems, give them the sympathy they crave, and are a shoulder to cry on. They even go so far as to send gifts to their targets to show they care, and this is one of the signs parents should watch for if they feel their child is at risk, and will be discussed in Chapter 9 of this book.

Predators will spend all of their time on the net, searching, talking, fantasizing and building their knowledge. They learn from each other, and they continue to expand their knowledge and their craft, and it is my personal mission to make it very hard for them to victimize any more children. If by writing this  book one child takes their information off of a page, or decides not to put up their information then that is one less child who is vulnerable, and that makes it all worthwhile.

Just like pedophiles that hang out near parks, or schools, online predators will hang out in chat rooms, read message boards, and pretend to be teens looking for a good friend. The same reason my job working undercover was easy at times is the same reason predators find it easy online. Building that rapport site unseen is a snap. We tend to get a good vibe or impression from someone's appearance by meeting them face-to-face but online all we have to judge by is text. Not their voice, or how they look or even smell, just their text. I would build a rapport with the bad guys online first which made it very easy to meet them in person and pretend I was a pedophile. That rapport was already built so when we met each other it was like we had known each other for years. If I would just meet them face-to-face first it would be a lot harder to do. I would have to convince by my words, my look and how I carried myself.

I could also be many different people online. I would talk to the same bad guy as numerous different people to gain different information about my suspect and I know they do the same with children online. They're sneaky (like I was) but they can be beat, and how we do that is by knowing how they work and by not giving them that ammunition to get at our children.

Grooming their targets when the time is right is like taking little steps to see what they can get away with, or what their victims feel comfortable doing. For example, they may send a picture to the victim of a child with his or her clothes on. They later send a file with the same child in more of a suggestive pose. As their relationship online grows, then there are images sent with pornography and each time the predator sees the reactions of the child to know if they can go further or if they should take it a little easier. They will eventually engage in explicit sexual discussions. They may even have their victims do things to themselves, possibly take pictures of it, or say things very suggestive to them. This is also how they build up to a face-to-face meeting.

Now you might ask who are these people? Are they the dirty old men at the street corners wearing trench coats? The answer is NO! I always say, they are your next-door neighbours, your schoolteachers, your doctors, your lawyers, and community leaders.

I read a book that gave profiles for these types of individuals and I wanted to call the author to ask where she got her information because there is no set profile for the pedophile. There are certain traits they may have, like usually surrounding themselves in an occupation that deals with children, or some may be loners who have terrible personal skills but the fact is there is no real way to tell other than catching them and letting the world know. In my career I had arrested doctors, dentists, lawyers, schoolteachers, principals, labourers, journalists, businessmen, daycare owners, karate teachers, students, pizza delivery guys and many more different types of individuals. The one thing I can say is I never arrested a woman. There is the odd case which involves women, however they are very publicized in the news and they are usually schoolteachers involved with one of their students, so I am not saying it never occurs.

I stress all of this because on or off the net we have to be aware so we do not let our guard down; and we must protect our children. Some of the most respected people on this planet have a dark side, and that side is having a sexual interest towards children.

I could write a whole book on pedophiles and how they work, how they think and what makes them tick but that is really not my expertise. I know how they act before they get caught, how they brag about their accomplishment with children and how they study and research to get better at luring. There are many psychiatrists who have written books on the mind of pedophiles and I don't want to claim to be an expert on how their mind works, I just want to make sure parents don't let that guard down because someone has a University degree or a prominent job in our society.

Hackers

These individuals basically just like to cause trouble. Although some of what they do is for financial gain, from my experience I have found that most hackers like to see just how far they can get. In other words what can they break into and what can they take. I will discuss hacker programs later in this book, but just be aware that the term hacker means individuals who can access data through computer systems and use that information for financial or personal gain. They can invade your privacy by gaining access to all the files on your computer. This would include bank account numbers, Visa numbers, social insurance numbers and whatever else they find useful.

 Children don't realize that hacking is a crime and many of our youth are involved in such activities. These activities are such things as hacking into a website and changing content or hacking into your personal computer at home and gaining access to personal and financial information. Important files and documents can be deleted from your computer by such invasions. This is another reason why having your own

personal computer in the open so you can see what your children are doing is important. We should also protect our children from getting in trouble with the law. I had done numerous investigations with young offenders doing such activities and it comes as a complete shock to the parents when we showed up at the door with a search warrant.

There are many different software applications out there that can help you protect your home computer from such attacks. Do some research on software applications you can use to make sure you are never the victim of a hacker.

Pornography

This is for sure a huge business on the Web, and the biggest problem is that our children are able to access it instantly. There are many cases where they click on a link thinking it is one thing (school project material) and it turns out to be a pornography site. I am  not even talking about the illegal material, just material for 18 or older that our children happen upon. The illegal material is another thing totally, and it is just as easy to access for anyone. Websites hosting pornography are in the millions, and if you add the USENET newsgroups in the mix for distributing pornography it is mind-boggling. I will touch on USENET later in this book, but it is one of the oldest forums on the Internet used to distribute pornography as well as Child Pornography and Obscene Material.

When it comes to websites, many of the creators of these sites give out free teaser images for people to see before gaining access to the actual site. In stores you cannot show covers of magazines or videos for children to see, yet on the Internet anyone can access a free look at pornography.

Pornography can also be traded through chat rooms, instant messaging programs and e-mail. It is not just the websites we have to worry about, it is every other way of transmitting data that parents should be aware of, and take steps so their children are not exposed to this type of information.

Inappropriate sites

Due to the Internet being unregulated there is much more than just pornography we should worry about online. Explicit violence sites are horrible to say the least and just seeing some of these images could really have an effect on our children. We don't let them go to "R" rated movies so we can't let them access these sites on the Internet either.

How-to sites are very big for kids to look at as well. How to build bombs, grow drugs or just about anything can be found on the Internet, including hate and racism sites. Research is great online but where there is information there could be very dangerous topics we have to be aware of. We have to make sure our children don't get caught up in what they can find out there in cyberspace.

Misinformation

Although we see the Internet as a great resource of information, the truth is there is a lot of misinformation out there. People tend to believe anything they read on the net. They receive e-mails of stories, or warnings about things that just are not true, or  they go searching for information and find sites that have it posted but have no idea that they are not fact.

Every Internet user can be a publisher by just having their own website or posting on a message board, and children can be misinformed on just about any subject. Children tend to believe anything they read and this can be very dangerous. There are sites explaining how to build a bomb, and I know of one individual personal who lost a hand trying to mimic the instructions from the Internet. All of this information, and misinformation, can be dangerous and we all have to be aware that not everything in writing is true.

Misinformation is extremely bothersome when it comes to doing homework or research online for a project. There is nothing worse than quoting information or studies that have never really occurred. Parents and children should always try to verify information they find, or make sure the site the information is posted on is a reputable one.

Privacy

Giving out our personal information is one thing, but it is another to have our computers do it for us. When we register on a site or fill in an online form on a website, cookies are held on our system and that information could be used by other sites or given to third parties to later contact you or send you spam e-mail. Filling out any online forms or questionnaires could be giving your information out to many, not just the one site you are on, and you should be aware of this. I am not saying you should never fill out forms or make purchases online (I order books online all the time), I am just making you aware that depending on the site you never know where this information goes. Make sure you research the site you are giving this information to. Make sure they are dependable and reputable before filling out any information or online form on their website. This is how a lot of business is done today, so the odds are you will be doing some sort of online purchase; just be sure to do it as safely as possible before doing so.

Spam

With the amount of advertisers and marketers on the net there is an increase in unwanted e-mails or "spam". According to the website www.whatis.com (which is a great resource for finding out internet terms and many other terms) the definition of "spam" is:

Spam is unsolicited e-mail on the Internet. (E-mail that is wanted is sometimes referred to as ham.) From the sender's point-of-view, spam is a form of bulk mail, often sent to a list obtained from a spambot or to a list obtained by companies that specialize in creating e-mail distribution lists. To the receiver, it usually seems like junk e-mail.

Spam is roughly equivalent to unsolicited telephone marketing calls except that the user pays for part of the message since everyone shares the cost of maintaining the Internet. Spammers typically send a piece of e-mail to a distribution list in the millions, expecting that only a tiny number of readers will respond to their offer. It has become a major problem for all Internet users.

Spam can be a real pain in the neck, however most Internet service providers offer some type of spam protection in your e-mail accounts and there are many different free software programs out there that can assist you in reducing the amount of spam that enters your e-mail inbox. Many anti-virus programs have a spam-guard built into them which checks your e-mails as they come in and determines if the e-mail is spam or not and will eliminate them from entering your inbox as well. My Internet service provider cuts down on this with their technology, and I also use anti-virus software that helps eliminate spam, but some messages still get through so I just delete them as they come. It is one of the pains we will have to live with using the Internet.

One year ago I received an e-mail that appeared to be from my bank. All the logos were there and the e-mail appeared to be coming from my financial institution, but I knew something was up; my bank has never contacted me via e-mail for the 20 years I have used them. Also the e-mail asked me to confirm my login information as there was a problem with their site and some data was lost. The link in the e-mail showed my bank site, but I knew something was up. I looked at the information contained in the e-mail (or the source) and it showed if I clicked that link I would be taken somewhere different on the Internet, not to the bank site. What these people who sent the e-mail did was set up a website somewhere and copied my banks site exactly. Everything looked the same as the website, but when you went to log in using your bank card number and password I would imagine nothing would happen because all they wanted was your card number and password which you would type in. This is called "Phishing" and is explained in Chapter 6 (Electronic Threats). I reported this and sure enough, thousands of people had received the e-mail. Now they did not get a list of clients or anything to send the e-mail to, they just sent it to as many e-mails as they could, hoping that some would be clients of the bank. I know this because I received another one shortly after with the same information but for another bank which I did not deal with. These types of scams can be very dangerous for everyone. Don't fall for e-mails you get that ask for any type of information such as login name or password.

Pop-ups

Pop-ups are the smaller sized Internet browsing windows that show up with some sort of advertisement or message. They can be extremely annoying and many browsers now have the option to block pop-up windows. According to www.whatis.com the definition of a pop-up is:

*A pop-up is a graphical user interface (**GUI**) display area, usually a small window,that suddenly appears ("pops up") in the foreground of* *the visual interface. Pop-ups can be initiated by a single or double mouse click or* **rollover** *(sometimes called a mouseover), and also possibly by voice command or can simply be timed to occur. A pop-up window must be smaller than the background window or interface; otherwise, it's a replacement interface.*

Pop-up Ads are just a little different and a little more annoying. The definition of pop-up ads according to www.whatis.com is the following"

A pop-up ad is a pop-up window used for advertising. When the program is initiated by some user action, such as a mouse click or a mouseover, a window containing an offer for some product or service appears in the foreground of the visual interface. Like all pop-ups, a pop-up ad is smaller than the background interface - windows that fill the user interface are called replacement interfaces - and usually resembles a small browser window with only the close, minimize, and maximize options at the top. A variation on the pop-up ad, the pop-under, is a window that loads behind the Web page that you're viewing, only to appear when you leave that Web site.

Pop-up ads are not popular with the average Web surfer, and there are several products that disable them, such as Pop-up Stopper, Pop-up Killer, and Pop-up Annihilator. One thing to look for in such a program is the ability to differentiate between user-initiated pop-up windows and others, because many other applications (such as Webcasts, for example) make use of pop-up windows. If a pop-up stopper utility can't tell the difference between a pop-up window that the user has requested and an unsought pop-up ad, the program may cause more problems for the user than it solves.

The problem with many of these is if you click on the pop-up it takes you to sites which are hard to get out of because every time you try and exit another screen pops up and so on and so on. My recommendation is to have the pop-up blocker on in your Internet browser or find the appropriate software to help eliminate pop-ups.

Viruses

Viruses are just as they sound like – an infection on your computer. It is a special code contained within a computer program that is designed to infect a file on your computer when executed. The following is a definition from TechTarget.com:

 *In computers, a virus is a program or programming code that replicates by being copied or initiating its copying to another program, computer boot sector or document. Viruses can be transmitted as attachments to an e-mail note or in a downloaded file, or be present on a diskette or CD. The immediate source of the e-mail note, downloaded file, or diskette you've received is usually unaware that it contains a virus. Some viruses wreak their effect as soon as their code is executed; other viruses lie dormant until circumstances cause their code to be executed by the computer. Some viruses are benign or playful in intent and effect ("Happy Birthday, Ludwig!") and some can be quite harmful, erasing data or causing your hard disk to require reformatting. A virus that replicates itself by resending itself as an e-mail attachment or as part of a network message is known as a worm.*

A worm is:

In a computer, a worm is a self-replicating virus that does not alter files but resides in active memory and duplicates itself. Worms use parts of an operating system that are automatic and usually invisible to the user. It is common for worms to be noticed only when their uncontrolled replication consumes system resources, slowing or halting other tasks.

I have been a victim of these at one time or another but now I use security software to help prevent these attacks on my computer. As stated before, these programs will be discussed in a later chapter in this book.

To avoid viruses, I suggest some good network security software and to use it on each boot-up of your computer as well as filter any e-mails you receive, and programs or documents you download from the Internet. You should also scan any and all disks that you put in your floppy drive or CD ROM. Scan anything that contains data if you are not aware of its origin.

Flaming

You may hear the term "flaming" around the house if you have children on the Internet. Flaming is what I like to call bad-mouthing in cyber-space. If your children are in a chat room or if they post on message boards, they may have been "flamed" at one time or another.

As the definition explains below it is a verbal lashing in public. Let your children know that this type of behavior is unwanted and should not be done to anyone.

Unfortunately this is how many of the cyber-bullying cases are started and it really can get out of control.

It is not pleasant to be flamed, but with children thinking they are totally anonymous on the Internet, it can really start to be a problem on message boards and chatrooms.

Here is the whatis.com definition of Flaming:

On the Internet, flaming is giving someone a verbal lashing in public. Often this is on a Usenet newsgroup but it could be on a Web forum or perhaps even as e-mail with copies to a distribution list. Unless in response to some rather obvious flamebait, flaming is poor netiquette. Certain issues tend to provoke emphatically stated responses, but flaming is often directed at a self-appointed expert rather than at the issues or information itself and is sometimes directed at unwitting but opinionated newbies who appear in a newsgroup.

Chapter Four

Children
On
The Net

*"Oh, what a tangled web do parents weave
when they think that their children are naive."*

Ogden Nash

Chapter 4

Children on the Net

Canadian studies have shown that the majority of elementary school children use the Internet to play games and for e-mail, and those in high school use the Internet for e-mail, chatting and music downloads. I have noticed from the children I have talked to during lectures that I conduct that elementary school students are using Chat Clients more often than in the past.

Table 4. What would you do on the Internet if you had an hour or two? YCWW II, 2005		
	Percent of respondents	
Activity	**Girls**	**Boys**
Talk to friends on instant messaging	62	43
Download music, listen to music	41	37
Play games – including multiplayer games	30	56
Write and read emails	15	5
Surf for fun	13	14
Visit a chat room	6	7
Do school work online	6	3
Get information or advice on a topic that I am interested in (not school work)	7	8
Work on my own Web site	6	4
Shop, or get information about things I might buy	3	4
Visit entertainment sites – movies, videos, etc.	4	7
Get news, weather, sports	1	5
Blogging, writing online diaries	2	1
Download movies, TV shows	3	5

Note: Percentages add to more than 100 as respondents could choose two options.

The days of using the telephone are almost all gone for children now that most homes have computers in them. My daughter is 9 years old and thinks she needs to use a chat program so she can talk to her friends from school.

Right now I don't believe it is appropriate, so she is the dinosaur of her class and the kids actually have to use a phone (imagine punching numbers into a box and holding this thing to your face).

Chat clients are used by many people, not just children. I have a couple of different companies and I use chat programs to talk to programmers overseas, clients in other cities and family members. It is cheap and with the technology now, voice conversations over the Internet are actually clearer than the telephone because it is digital. I will touch on the different chat clients and how e-mail works later on, but you should know that more and more children are getting on the Internet at younger and younger ages, so all of these different applications will be used more.

We have to come to terms that the Internet is here to stay and getting stronger day by day. Right now as I am typing this chapter, I am in my local library and the majority of computers (about 90%) are being used by teens and pre-teens and it appears most, if not all, have a chat application open and they are talking to people online.

Top ten favourite sites *YCWW II, 2005*		
Site	**Primary content**	**Percent who chose the site as one of their 3 favourites**
Addicting Games	games	18.2
Miniclip	games	16.3
Neopets	virtual pet site	9.8
eBaumsworld	humour: jokes, photos, animation	5.7
Newgrounds	flash animation, jokes	4.2
Runescape	an online game	4.2
Candystand	games	3.7
Funnyjunk	humour: jokes, photos, animation	3.7
YTV	TV channel info, games	3.3
Launch	streaming radio	3.3

Children also use the
Internet to play games.
The percentage is higher
for boys in this area as
they love to play video
games against other
children from around the

world. Computers are now faster, and made with gaming in
mind for kids. Now that high-speed is in the majority of
homes, it makes online gaming a big hit with the kids.
While playing some of these games you can communicate
with others with text or even voice over the Internet at the
same time, which makes the games even more interactive
for children. I am not into the games myself but a couple
of my nephews do use their computers for gaming, and
even hook up their TV driven videogames like PlayStation
to the Internet with a network cable hooked into their high-
speed Internet access. If they wear a headset and
microphone they can speak to others during the game,
which makes it extremely fun when you can speak to your
teammates in team games. I have tried it and it is a good
time.

The other major use for the Internet with children is to
download their favourite songs. The music industry has
expanded on the Internet over the past few years to the
point where now you can buy and download music on the
net. There are some risks to this however. People will
share out their music files in what is called a P2P Network
(Peer-to-Peer Network). This makes downloading fast as
you get bits and pieces of the song from different users at
the same time to increase the speed you receive the song.

 The problem is some people share out files that could have viruses in them or auto-dialing applications or what may be called modem hijacking. I will touch on these later in the book but I have been the victim of an auto-dialer, but caught it before it did any damage. When this file is executed (double-clicked or opened) it disconnects your modem from your phone line, picks it back up and dials a number with extremely high phone rates. It connects you back to the Internet via this phone number but if you don't hear your modem disconnect and dial back out you will see no disruption with your Internet and you keep surfing the net for hours while paying a huge price on your phone bill. It can also dial out if your computer is left on and idle for a lengthy period of time, then it just dials to this number when you are not around to shut it down. This does not occur with high-speed access because you will not have a phone line hooked up to dial into your Internet Service Provider. Spyware (which will be discussed later in this book) can also be downloaded with these files and is something to be aware of as well.

Table 3. Electronic devices that kids have
YCWW II, 2005

Device	Percent of respondents		
	I have one for my own personal use	I use one that other family members use too	I don't use this
MP3 player (iPod, Pocket DJ, etc.)	41	13	47
Computer that has Internet	37	57	4
Cell phone	23	45	32
Webcam	22	22	56
Computer that does not have Internet	12	14	74
PDA (Palm Pilot, Blackberry, etc.)	8	12	80
VOIP phone (over the Internet)	7	9	84
Pager	3	10	87

Note: Each row adds to 100 percent (within rounding error).

The electronic device used most by children is not a cell phone, or Walkman but an MP3 player. The downloads that take place online for music is usually in this format and that is why downloading music is one of the top uses for kids on the Internet. They can get their music for free and not have to pay for CD's. I am not going to get into the legal debate on downloading music for free, I am just simply stating that it does occur through P2P applications like LimeWire, Kaaza, Imesh, Bearshare, Morpheus, Audio Galaxy and many, many more. Most of these applications also let you download movies, which is on the rise with the increase of high-speed throughout our nation.

Most children have e-mail accounts and in a 2005 national study, it showed that over 85% of youth have their own personal e-mail account. E-mailing is another communication tool youth use the Internet for and I will explain the dangers of this later in this book. Free  e-mail accounts are everywhere on the Internet and signing up for them takes just seconds. There are dangers of course, and the files they receive from people could be dangerous or the content not appropriate for children.

Table 2. Do you have an email account? YCWW II, 2005	
Email account	Percent of respondents
Free account	72
School account	14
My own box on a family account	12
Share a family mailbox with others	10
None	14

Note: percentages add to more than 100 as some respondents have several email accounts.

Table 15. Visits to offensive sites by grade and gender Grades 7 - 11 YCWW II, 2005										
	GIRLS Grade					BOYS Grade				
Site	7	8	9	10	11	7	8	9	10	11
Accidental visits										
Porn sites *	12	12	16	14	10	26	24	29	24	21
Violence or gore sites * †	9	12	14	9	7	18	16	17	12	12
Gambling sites	11	12	13	12	8	14	16	14	11	10
Adult chat rooms ^	8	9	8	7	3	6	6	10	8	10
Hate sites	4	7	7	6	6	8	5	10	7	6
Purposeful visits										
Porn sites * †	1	4	3	8	7	12	19	31	36	33
Violence or gore sites * †	4	4	11	8	7	23	23	34	33	26
Gambling sites * †	3	4	5	7	8	9	13	19	20	25
Adult chat rooms * †	3	6	6	8	6	5	8	14	16	18
Hate sites * †	1	1	3	4	3	3	6	8	10	10

Note: Significant differences:
* = Gender: more boys than girls visit.
† = Grade: the proportion who visit changes with grade level.
^ = Gender by Grade: gender differences change with grade level

Another use for the Internet with our youth is to maintain their own website or blog site. To me these 2 terms are very close but the difference is a blog site is a site on the Internet where you can keep a daily journal or diary of everything you are doing. You can upload images for people to see there, share your music, or post your profile and links to your friend's web or blog sites. Blogging is relatively new but the explosion of this is making it very simple for children to get an account and start posting information about themselves with little or no technical skill whatsoever.

Table 11. Why do you pretend to be someone else? Grades 7 - 11 YCWW II, 2005	
Why did you pretend?	**Percent of respondents**
I want to see what it would be like to be someone else	28
I can pretend to be older and talk to older kids	28
I can flirt with people	26
I can act mean to people and not get into trouble	17
Other reasons	53

Note: Percentages add to more than 100 as respondents could choose several reasons.
Results exclude the 41 percent of respondents who have never pretended to be someone else online.

Children on the Net

As parents we have to start getting involved, but in order to do this we need to know what our kids are using the Internet for, and understand a little bit about how these applications work.

Table 14. In this school year (since September 2004) have you visited these sites? Grades 7 - 11 YCWW IL 2005			
Site	On purpose	By accident	Never
Porn sites	16	19	66
Violence or gore sites	18	12	70
Gambling sites	12	12	76
Adult chat rooms	9	8	83
Hate sites (against different races or religions. e.g. Neo-Nazi sites)	5	7	89
Any of these sites	34	35	31

Chapter Five

Uses of the Internet

"Misery is when grown-ups don't realize how miserable kids can feel."

Suzanne Heller

Chapter 5

Uses of the Internet

As I mentioned in the beginning of this book, there are many different uses for the Internet. Most people think of just websites, which is only a part of the Internet itself. I am going to cover some of the more common uses in this chapter of the book so when parents hear their children talking about them, they will have some knowledge on not only what it is, but how it works as well.

Web Browsing (Surfing the Net)

This is referred to as 'surfing the Net'. Browsing the Internet is going on the World Wide Web or the 'www' you always hear about. If you go  to my website you would have to open your Internet browser (there are many – Internet Explorer, Netscape, Firefox) and type in the address or URL (Uniform Resource Locator) www.cyber-safety.com. Typically, a web URL is prefixed with "http://". This tells the web browser how to access the information contained at that address. HTTP stands for "Hyper Text Transfer Protocol" or a website.

 The "www" is the name of the system or computer that hosts the website. Not all sites need this in front but it indicates that the website is part of the World Wide Web. "cyber-safety" is my domain, or address. I own this name and it is my home on the Internet. The ".com" is the type of website, in my case meaning commercial organization. There is ".net" which means network, ".ca" that stands for Canada, ".org" for nonprofit organizations, and ".gov" for government agencies, and different ones popping up every so often to expand the addressing system. For a full list and what they mean, just do a search on the net. (You will notice through this book – I am not going to give you everything, otherwise this book would be 3000 pages and I just don't have the time; besides, work on getting used to the net, as I will explain later that part of safety is getting comfortable and going on the net with your kids to see what they are doing.)

Website surfing can be dangerous because of what your children could come across. Remember the Internet is not regulated. There are hundreds of thousands of websites (probably millions) with inappropriate material on them. These sites don't have any way to really verify age. Most will give you free samples of pornography to see if you like it, without verifying age. There are sites on how to build explosives, and how to hack other people's computers, so we have to make sure our children are not accessing these sites. There are dangers in just surfing.

Search Engines

There are so many websites on the Internet that finding the one that best suits you or that you are looking for can be difficult. That is why most people use some type of search engine to find the site(s) that meets their needs.

A search engine allows you to conduct a search on a topic of interest or the information you are looking for using keywords or other criteria. You would first go to a search  engine site such as google (www.google.com or www.google.ca) and in the search area type in what you are looking for and hit the search button, and a listing of sites will appear that have your topic or your keyword within the site.

There are two different type of search engines; directory based or those that use keywords. Directories will organize the results by subject, and may provide a description. The keyword-based engine will generate a list of websites according to the words you type.

Google is known for its keyword search ability, (just go there and type Rob Nickel and see what appears) whereas Yahoo is a directory-based system. Results are similar; they just go about it differently. There are many different search engines and everyone has their preference in regards to searching on the Internet. Find the engine you like and get to know some others. You may be surprised at how different they really can be.

Here is the whatis.com definition for Search Engines:

On the Internet, a search engine is a coordinated set of programs that includes:

- *A spider (also called a "crawler" or a "bot") that goes to every page or representative pages on every Web site that wants to be searchable and reads it, using hypertext links on each page to discover and read a site's other pages*
- *A program that creates a huge index (sometimes called a "catalog") from the pages that have been read*
- *A program that receives your search request, compares it to the entries in the index, and returns results to you*

An alternative to using a search engine is to explore a structured directory of topics. Yahoo, which also lets you use its search engine, is the most widely-used directory on the Web. A number of Web portal sites offer both the search engine and directory approaches to finding information.

Blogging (A Daily Journal Website)

 Blogging is one of the newest crazes on the Internet. This is a daily log or journal that people keep. It is found as a web page on the Internet but is quick and easy to update. Children find this a great place to express themselves and let others know what they are up to, how they are feeling, and what they did that day; but there are other uses for this

site as well. They can have a community message board hooked into them so people can leave their comments. They can post their favourite links to other websites as well as post pictures in a gallery for others to see.

These blog sites are very similar to profiles for instant messaging programs on the Internet but have become more popular because of their numerous options. It is a personal website for anyone, for no fee, and they are becoming a way for others to gather information, and either bully or target our children.

The fact is, it is now part of the Internet and we can't stop our children from going onto these sites and having one of their own, but we can let them know what information is appropriate and should not be posted on their blog.

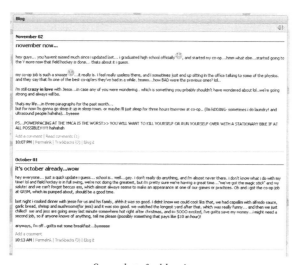

Screenshot of a blog site.

Some of the dangers that children don't think about when posting information in their profile or on their blog site, are little things like "Pictures of our vacation December 18th to

told the whole world when you take vacation, when your house is empty, when someone can break in and be relatively sure nobody is at home. I think of these things because I had to think like the bad guy for 7 years, but most children don't know, and trust me when I say the bad guys do look for these things. Believe it or not there are other children your kids go to school with who break into houses. Don't be naive in thinking this will never happen or kids like that don't go to our schools because they do!

My niece had similar information on a website she had and I found it. Her parents had no idea she even had a website, let alone pictures posted of their vacation with the dates they were gone.

Any ammunition that is out there for others to see is not a good idea. Pictures of our children with their personal information posted is just asking for trouble if the wrong people are accessing it, and remember it is out there for the whole world to see. Also keep in mind that once it is on the net it is archived for years. I can still pull up an old website I had posted back in 2001, yet I took it off the net over 4 years ago. Information can always be gathered if you know where to look, and blog sites are no different.

E-Mail (Electronic Mail)

Most people know e-mail by this day and age. Most people use it at work, and the majority use it from home, and the simple fact is we cannot get away from it; e-mail is here to stay. E-mail is a computer or electronic version

is here to stay. E-mail is a computer or electronic version of postal mail. Each message has a return address to you and an address to where it is going. My e-mail is rob@cyber-safety.com and is unique to me because it comes to my address "cyber-safety.com" and is addressed to me, "rob". If you send a message to "kim@cyber-safety.com" it would come to my address, but to my wife Kim's account. Remember more than one person can live at an address, so you have to make sure not only the address is right but the person on the address is correct. A great example of an e-mail address that a lot of kids have is "theirname@hotmail.com". Hotmail is one of hundreds of free e-mail services that children can sign up with. Hotmail is a favourite because you will also get an MSN passport with it so you can talk on MSN Messenger (discussed later in this book) and space for a profile for your friends to view, as well as a blog site so you can keep your journal up to date. Hotmail is also a favourite because it has been around for a very long time. If you put this book down right now and ask your child what their hotmail address is, I am sure you will be shocked when your kids say "how did you know I had a hotmail account, have you been spying?"

There are many different security issues with e-mail that I will touch on later in this book, but for now just remember that e-mail is one of the most popular uses of the Internet. Billions of e-mails are sent every day in the world; it is the main system of communication in the world.

Mailing Lists

A mailing list is composed of a group of people who receive e-mail messages on a particular topic, and there are different types of lists that are used on the Internet.

An announcement list would be used for things such as product announcements or specials that a particular company would send out to people who have registered with their site. For example, I do a lot of shopping at Future Shop, so I registered on their website. About once a week I receive an e-mail about specials they have going on at the time. You cannot reply to these e-mails or talk with others who are on this list. You can however unsubscribe from the list as they usually have a link at the bottom of the e-mail you just click to be removed and never receive any further correspondence.

There are also open discussion lists, meaning everyone on the list can send e-mails to the entire list. These are usually used for subjects like cancer survivors, or hobbies or interests so a discussion can take place. Hence the name "Discussion List."

A moderated discussion list is similar to the open discussion list except when you send an e-mail to the entire list, the person in charge of setting up the list will view the e-mail before it goes to the list and decides whether it should go out or not. Both open and moderated lists usually have an option to unsubscribe from them. I belong to a few, and if I find myself not reading them or losing interest I just unsubscribe from them.

Children might subscribe to any one of these 3 types of lists if they have an interest in a certain area. So if you see your child's e-mail box you may notice e-mails from mailing lists.

Here is the whatis.com definition of Mailing List:

A mailing list is a list of people who subscribe to a periodic mailing distribution on a particular topic. On the Internet, mailing lists include each person's e-mail address rather than a postal address. Mailing lists have become a popular way for Internet users to keep up with topics they're interested in. Many software producers and other vendors are now using them as a way to keep in touch with customers.

Newsgroups (Usenet)

This is not a huge player in the world of children on the Internet but you still may hear rumblings about it around the house. A newsgroup is like an assortment of bulletin boards where people can post messages on the boards that are of interest to them. These boards are sectioned into topic-specific categories and you can read other peoples posts, respond to them, and upload images or files to them. These messages are sent or "posted" much like sending an e-mail. Newsgroups are not as popular as they were 10 years ago, but they are still in existence and can contain inappropriate material for children, like pornography. To view newsgroups you need a news reader application that can be found online for free or it may be included with your operating system like Microsoft Windows, which has Microsoft Outlook Newsreader bundled with it. You can also use the Google website to view newsgroup postings by going to "http://groups.google.com". There are many different categories for newsgroups that are listed below:

Alt - Alternative (where most inappropriate material is found)
Misc - Miscellaneous
News - Usenet News
Rec - Recreational Activities
Sci - Scientific Issues

Soc - Social Issues

Talk - Controversial Social and Cultural Issues

Newsgroups are used by many criminals looking for victims. This is a place where they can gather information on "posters" in the newsgroups.

Screen shot of what a newsgroup looks like.

I relayed a story about making a phone call to a man who wanted to talk to my daughter and the female undercover officer was questioned about the Spice Girls. This investigation actually started with a newsgroup posting. He posted in a newsgroup looking for people who were interested in incest. I replied to this posting and the investigation started from there. We did learn that this individual was sexually assaulting his own daughter, and the investigation was very successful.

In the Child Pornography Section we conducted many more investigations stemming from newsgroup postings. A few of these investigations were from Young Offenders posting child pornography or threatening others in certain newsgroups. For more information on newsgroups and how to access them just take a look at the google address I provided and you will have a better understanding.

Here is the whatis.com definition of Newsgroups:

A newsgroup is a discussion about a particular subject consisting of notes written to a central Internet site and redistributed through Usenet, a worldwide network of news discussion groups. Usenet uses the Network News Transfer Protocol (NNTP).

Newsgroups are organized into subject hierarchies, with the first few letters of the newsgroup name indicating the major subject category and sub-categories represented by a subtopic name. Many subjects have multiple levels of subtopics. Some major subject categories are: news, rec (recreation), soc (society), sci (science), comp (computers), and so forth (there are many more). Users can post to existing newsgroups, respond to previous posts, and create new newsgroups.

Newcomers to newsgroups are requested to learn basic Usenet netiquette and to get familiar with a newsgroup before posting to it. A frequently asked questions is provided. The rules can be found when you start to enter the Usenet through your browser or an online service. You can subscribe to the postings on a particular newsgroup.

Some newsgroups are moderated by a designated person who decides which postings to allow or to remove. Most newsgroups are unmoderated.

Message Boards/Discussion Boards

A message board is exactly like a newsgroup but can be viewed with a web browser and will be operated from a website, so you do not need to set up a newsreader application to access, just an Internet connection and web browser. Some boards require you to register before you can access the site, but others are wide open so you can go in and read about the topics. An example of an online message board would be Yahoo! Groups found at http://groups.yahoo.com.

Reproduced with permission of Yahoo! Inc. © 2006 by Yahoo! Inc. YAHOO! And the YAHOO! Logo are trademarks of Yahoo! Inc.

Here is the whatis.com definition of Discussion Boards:

A discussion board (known also by various other names such as discussion group, discussion forum, message board, and online forum) is a general term for any online "bulletin board" where you can leave and expect to see responses to messages you have left. Or you can just read the board. The first discussion boards were available on bulletin board systems. On the Internet, Usenet provides thousands of discussion boards; these can now sometimes be viewed from a Web browser.

Today, many Web sites, including Whatis.com and other TechTarget.com sites, offer a discussion board so that users can share and discuss information and opinions. Special software is available that provides discussion board capability for a Web site.

Chat Rooms

This is the place to hang out, have fun, and get in trouble. Chat rooms are fun for kids because they can go in, talk to people they don't know, and feel like they are untouchable. They think that because the Internet does not require your real name, they are totally anonymous, which is a little true but not totally. How do you think I caught bad guys for 7 years online? Chat rooms are run by different services and websites. They have come so far in the last few years that anyone can put a chat room on their personal site in just a couple of minutes. The chat rooms I will discuss are the popular chat rooms like Yahoo, ICQ, Internet Relay Chat and others.

Chat rooms are just what they sound like, rooms where you can go to chat with others. These are not personal one-on-one chats (although the option is always there to do private chats) but group chats with as many people in the room as granted by the provider or moderator of the room. Take Yahoo chat rooms for example. There is a section for teens and there could be hundreds of rooms to choose from. When you enter the room you will see nicknames listed on one side and in the main window the conversations in text. Yahoo also allows voice in the room so you can also hear people using their computer microphones to talk in the room. Video chats are also accepted but need to be on a one-on-one basis. There are other video chat rooms that will allow multiple people, and you can see many people on video screens on your computer.

Different things can happen in these rooms, files can be traded between people, but more importantly, information can be exchanged - personal information which is where a lot of kids get into trouble. This is where a lot of the cyber-bullying starts. Kids get carried away in chat rooms and spout off because they think they are "anonymous", but like I stated before that is not really the case.

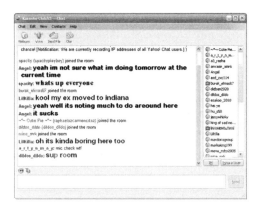

Reproduced with permission of Yahoo! Inc. © 2006 by Yahoo! Inc. YAHOO! And the YAHOO! Logo are trademarks of Yahoo! Inc.

Right now typing in my hometown library I can see one young girl talking in a yahoo chat room. There is at least 30 people in that room and the messages are flying by fast. I am sure many parents have noticed just how fast our children can type. I am not saying we should ban our children from these rooms but they have to know which ones are appropriate and which ones are not. When I do my lectures on Internet safety I show a live demonstration on a yahoo chat room to show how they work. For this demonstration it took me 2 hours to get the live video footage of my computer screen, not because it was not clear, or because of technical difficulties, but because I wanted a 30 second clip without any swearing, or rude remarks. With the audio chatting kids get in there and let loose. Many have no respect for the other people in the room and as parents you have to determine if that is a place you would like your children to hang out.

Children can be easily offended by remarks said in these chat room communities. Words do hurt and cyber-bullying is not fun at all.

On one investigation I talked with a young girl who got a little carried away and "spouted off" in a chat room. The person she spouted off to found out her e-mail address from her profile, found her personal website, and all the links to this young girls friends online guest books. Later that day there were postings in these guest books about this young girl that were not very flattering, and it devastated her to the point where she did not want to go back to school. In another investigation, a girl thought it would be fun to tell the chat room and people in it that she had been raped by her father. I received the call and tracked down the young girl, spending hours online and on the phone to the local police agency, only to find they interviewed the girl and it was all a story to have some fun in the chat channel. Hours of police work wasted because she was having fun and sent myself, along with other law enforcement personnel on a wild goose chase.

IRC (Internet Relay Chat) Network

The IRC is the place to be! This was the motto in the Child Pornography section as this was the place where most of our cases stemmed from. In simple terms the IRC is a network of servers connected to the Internet and the sole purpose is for chatting and exchanging files. Once you log into one of these servers you are connected to the other servers in the network with other clients on them. You can create your own channel for talking with others (channel being the same as a room in regular chatting) and it is extremely easy to exchange files with others by using simple commands.

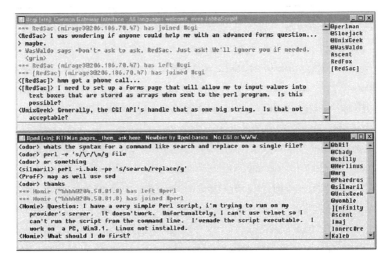

Screenshot of IRC Channels

Child pornography trading is big here because others can allow you access to the files on their hard drive (or collections of child pornography) by simply typing in a command and granting you access. Most FServers (File Servers) are set up for a give-take ratio. In other words, for every bite you send them in files you receive 2 bites of

90

downloading credit. This builds their collections of child pornography and when it is set up the person running the file server does not even have to be there, it is all automated.

On one investigation I had an individual with a huge collection of child pornography yet he left his house at 4 a.m. and did not get back from work until 9 p.m.. His collection was huge because he had his FServer running all day long while he was at work. He would come home to thousands of new files on his computer.

The IRC was also a place for pedophiles to congregate and talk with others who had a sexual interest for children. They would start channels call "littlegirlsexchat" for example and you could join and trade secrets, build relationships, and trade child pornography. They can also make private channels that are hidden, and only those who know the channel name and password were granted access, but the majority of channels are listed for all to see and they do not hide the fact of what their interest is. I was shocked in 1996 when I started working online at just how blatant they were and how easily they would let people have access to these files. Some would just let you have free access to their FServers, and others would give you so many free "credits" for download to give you a taste of what they had to offer. Children on IRC should be very careful and to be honest, I would not recommend the IRC to any children. There is just enough bad stuff on there to justify not going there. Yes there are channels devoted to other things but why have your children in any place that could be that dangerous?

Here is the whatis.com definition for IRC:

Internet Relay Chat (IRC) is a system for chatting that involves a set of rules and conventions and client/server software. On the Web, certain sites such as Talk City or IRC networks such as the Undernet provide servers and help you download an IRC client to your PC. Talk City also offers an IRC client applet that it downloads for you as part of their home page so that you can start chatting right away.

You can start a chat group (called a channel) or join an existing one. There is a protocol for discovering existing chat groups and their members. Depending on the type of network, nicknames can be reserved (registered) or just used during the session. Some channels encourage you to register a nickname that you always use and even offer space for a personal profile, picture, and personal home page link.

Popular ongoing IRC channels are #hottub and #riskybus. A number of channels are set up and conducted in foreign languages. The most common IRC networks are IRCnet (mostly European), EFnet (mostly North American), Undernet, and Dalnet. Popular IRC clients include mIRC for Windows, IRCle for Mac OS, and irc2 (the original client) for UNIX-base operating systems.

The IRC protocol uses Transmission Control Protocol (you can IRC via a Telnet client), usually on port 6667.

Instant Messaging

Instant messaging is the new telephone for children. Nobody uses the phone anymore; they are on MSN, ICQ, AOL, Yahoo, and a whole bunch of other letters you have probably never heard of. When I first started working undercover the Instant message service of choice was ICQ (standing for I Seek You). Now kids use the most popular MSN to chat with friends. If you have a teenager and they are not on MSN, I would be amazed. The reason it is so popular is because you can chat with text, voice, or video and you can send pictures or documents for school, but even better you can add others to your conversations. You can have your own private chat room with your friends.

The bad news is the bad guys use MSN as well. They could pose as children, and of course they set their profile and their life story to suit their target. I will give you an example:

In a case with the Child Pornography Section I met with a guy at a coffee shop who was telling me about luring children on the net. He explained to me that the easiest way to build a bond or rapport with a victim is to gather all the information you can on them. Find out what chat groups they belong to, what message boards they post on, read their profiles and gather information they post about their friends, and from that create someone they would have interest in. He said it was easy to find the loners, and ones that needed attention because they would flat-out post that they were loners, and didn't have many friends. I would do this type of education myself but I would tailor myself to what the bad guy's interest were. In other words, if I knew his interest was young boys I would now be a father of a young boy in the age range that individual prefers. Because the Internet can hide your identity to some degree it is very easy to pretend to be someone else and trick children into buying your story, and later working your magic to lure them to meet. Building a bond on the Internet is extremely easy. During my lectures I joke that you can't really pick up the phone and dial any number and just start talking to the person for no reason, and build a bond. People would think you are crazy! Yet on the

Internet people log on and join a chat room and just start talking to people they do not know. And because there is no looks involved (most of the time – no pictures or video – just text) there is no way to really judge a person. All you have to go by is the way they type. As funny as that sounds it is true. I could build a bond with the bad guy very easily as well because of this. I had done undercover work before the online work with the Child Pornography Section, and I have to admit, building that bond online was a piece of cake compared to meeting a drug dealer face-to-face. I would love to say it was tough and I was this great cop, but truthfully it was easy because all you had to work with was the written word, and if you knew the lingo, and how to peak their interest, it was pretty smooth sailing.

Keep this in mind when communicating with your children on the dangers of the Internet. Not everyone they are talking to is who they say they are. Even the majority of children I have surveyed in presentations have admitted to pretending to be someone else online, to trick people because they thought it was fun.

Screen shots of Yahoo, MSN and AOL Instant Messaging Applications

Chat programs are user-friendly, and kids love them but they are also a place where the predators like to build that bond. Children should not be talking to people they do not know on the Internet. This is a major rule, please never forget it.

P2P (Peer-to-Peer) File Sharing

Peer-to-Peer file sharing is mostly used for sharing music files or movies. Any type of file can be shared using most of these networks but the majority of children use these systems for their favourite music files, or if they have high speed service, for downloading the latest DVD releases – or ones not even on the market yet.

Here is the whatis.com definition of P2P:

1) Peer-to-peer is a communications model in which each party has the same capabilities and either party can initiate a communication session. Other models with which it might be contrasted include the client/server model and the master/slave model. In some cases, peer-to-peer communications is implemented by giving each communication node both server and client capabilities. In recent usage, peer-to-peer has come to describe applications in which users can use the Internet to exchange files with each other directly or through a mediating server.

IBM's Advanced Peer-to-Peer Networking (APPN) is an example of a product that supports the peer-to-peer communication model.

2) On the Internet, peer-to-peer (referred to as P2P) is a type of transient Internet network that allows a group of computer users with the same networking program to connect with each other and directly access files from one another's hard drives. Napster and Gnutella are examples of this kind of peer-to-peer software. Major producers of content, including record companies, have shown their concern about what they consider illegal sharing of copyrighted content by suing some P2P users.

Meanwhile, corporations are looking at the advantages of using P2P as a way for employees to share files without the expense involved in maintaining a centralized server and as a way for businesses to exchange information with each other directly.

How Does Internet P2P Work?

The user must first download and execute a peer-to-peer networking program. (Gnutellanet is currently one of the most popular of these decentralized P2P programs because it allows users to exchange all types of files.) After launching the program, the user enters the IP address of another computer belonging to the network. (Typically, the Web page where the user got the download will list several IP addresses as places to begin). Once the computer finds another network member on-line, it will connect to that user's connection (who has gotten their IP address from another user's connection and so on).

Users can choose how many member connections to seek at one time and determine which files they wish to share or password protect.

FTP (File Transfer Protocol)

File Transfer Protocol (FTP) is the easiest and usually the fastest way to transfer files from one computer to another on the Internet. I use FTP in my company mostly to upload (or put onto servers) websites my company creates for other companies, however it is used in exchanging files over the net between people. You could set your computer up with an FTP site for exchanging files with others and it is similar to FServers on the IRC Network. It is used in transferring child pornography as well as pirated software, movies, and music.

Although this is something that is not used a lot by children I thought I should explain it in this book in case the odd parent hears it mentioned and wants to know exactly what it is and what it is capable of doing.

There are many different software applications available on the Internet (some free of charge) and when the application is open you establish a connection with the other FTP site you will usually see your computer hard drive or FTP directory on one side of the screen, and the host (other FTP server) on the other side. From here all you have to do is choose a file, or multiple files on your computer and upload it to the other site by hitting an arrow button, or transfer button, and vise versa if you want to download a file from the FTP you are connected to. Even Windows Explorer or Internet Explorer is capable of connecting to FTP by typing in ftp.hostsite.com instead of www.hotsite.com and you will usually be asked for a username and password to connect to it. Then it is just a directory listing with the files, so you can upload and download.

Using FTP was a common occurrence in the Child Pornography Section because again, it was easy, fast and could be set up to use a credit system for the exchange of child pornography.

Here is the whatis.com definition of FTP:

File Transfer Protocol (FTP), a standard Internet protocol, is the simplest way to exchange files between computers on the Internet. Like the Hypertext Transfer Protocol (HTTP), which transfers displayable Web pages and related files, and the Simple Mail Transfer Protocol (SMTP), which transfers e-mail, FTP is an application protocol that uses the Internet's TCP/IP protocols. FTP is commonly used to transfer Web page files from their creator to the computer that acts as their server for everyone on the Internet. It's also commonly used to download programs and other files to your computer from other servers.

As a user, you can use FTP with a simple command line interface (for example, from the Windows MS-DOS Prompt window) or with a commercial program that offers a graphical user interface. Your Web browser can also make FTP requests to download programs you select from a Web page. Using FTP, you can also update (delete, rename, move, and copy) files at a server. You need to logon to an FTP server. However, publicly available files are easily accessed using anonymous FTP.

Basic FTP support is usually provided as part of a suite of programs that come with TCP/IP. However, any FTP client program with a graphical user interface usually must be downloaded from the company that makes it.

Chapter Six

Electronic
Threats

"The test of the morality of a society is what it does for its children."

Dietrich Bonhoeffer

Chapter 6

Electronic Threats

Ok, so we know about the bad guys on the other end a little, and how they can gather information on your children, but what about threats to our computers? What about hacking, viruses and invasion of my privacy? Well there is plenty of that as well.

I will not get too into detail on the electronic threats, but you should be made aware of their existence. These threats have to do with your computer and their files, and what happens when opening documents or clicking on certain areas on a website, that in turn can harm your system, and your privacy.

Most people have heard of a virus on computers, probably because one is in the news every other day. But, I am going to expand on other electronic threats so you have a reference to go by when you hear something other than "Virus".

Trojan Programs

When I was with the Child Pornography Section we received many calls about these types of investigations because at first there was no electronic crime section. We were the only section of the OPP who had computers and knew a little about the Internet. I had my eyes opened

pretty fast about how people can get into your computer, and actually take control of it. I had to do some research on Trojan software, which is exactly what it sounds like, a Trojan horse, that is put into your computer then opened and the bad guy takes over. Trojan programs, when executed on your system, open a back door where hackers can break into your computer. The file that is executed may look harmless, like a picture file, zip file, or an application, but when executed (clicked), it installs and embeds itself all over your system. All a hacker needs now is that you are online, and they have a direct connection into your computer where they can not only look at your files, but see what you are typing at that time, see what is on your screen, and activate your microphone to the computer as well as any camera attached to your computer. They could shut down your computer, or open the CD drive or just start executing files on your system to drive you crazy. This would be one of the major reasons children should not have computers in their rooms.

One investigation we conducted was extremely scary. I received a call from a concerned mother who told the following story:

"My daughter was on her computer in her room and was talking to a boy she met online. The boy said he sent a picture of himself in an e-mail to her but when she clicked on the image nothing happened. She asked the boy why she could not see his picture, and he said there must be something wrong with her e-mail. Then he said "but I really like that red sweater you are wearing!" My daughter never told him that information and she just figured it was a good guess but called me into the room to read this conversation. When I leaned over to read the screen a message came up that said "Your mom is really hot too, I like her cleavage." I knew right then he could see through our camera and I shut down our system."

When her computer was scanned it showed her daughter executed a Trojan program when she clicked on the attachment thought to be a picture of the boy.

A similar case we investigated had much the same details except it ruined a young girls life. She received and executed a Trojan program much the same way, by thinking it was a picture of a boy she met on the net, and when he took over the computer he played hardball. He told her he would totally destroy all files on the computer so her father and mother would lose all of their files if she did not take a picture of herself naked and send to him. The girl refused thinking he had no control over anything, then the words "BYE" showed on the screen and the computer shut off. She restarted the computer and as soon as a connection to the Internet took place another message popped up saying "see I told you – I can do anything.... Watch your CD drive" and when she looked down it opened without her touching a button. This girl had been in trouble with her parents because a virus got onto the computer before from a download and she did not want to get into any more trouble so she took the picture and sent it to the boy. Within minutes this picture showed up on all of the girl's friends web page guest books, and this girl could not return to the school because of the embarrassment she had been through. The boy then started asking for more pictures

103

from the waist down, and she refused and told her parents. I eventually tracked down who this individual was and it was a 15-year-old boy who had done this to about 23 girls. He had made life very difficult for them, and really only got a slap on the wrist for doing these things. Trojans are powerful and scary things that we have to be aware of. We tell our children not to talk to strangers and not to accept things from strangers yet they are online talking to people they do not know and opening attachments in e-mails, or in instant messages from people they do not know. Make sure your children know about Trojans, and to suspect any attachments to have one in them.

Most virus protection software will detect Trojans as well, so make sure the software you use to keep your computer virus-free also has the ability to detect Trojans and that it is updated regularly.

Viruses

Viruses are not the same as Trojan Programs. A virus contains "payloads," which are instructions that cause damage to your computer in some way. These infect your system in different ways, ranging from deleting certain files, sending confidential information to another computer, or just plain wreaking havoc by sending corrupting files so nothing really works right on your computer. Viruses can be housed in basically any type of file. It is destructive in nature, and attaches itself to a legitimate program to replicate itself.

Here is the whatis.com definition of Virus:

In computers, a virus is a program or programming code that replicates by being copied or initiating its copying to another program, computer boot sector or document. Viruses can be transmitted as attachments to an e-mail note or in a downloaded file, or be present on a diskette or CD. The immediate source of the e-mail note, downloaded file, or diskette you've received is usually unaware that it contains a virus. Some viruses wreak their effect as soon as their code is executed; other viruses lie dormant until circumstances cause their code to be executed by the computer. Some viruses are benign or playful in intent and effect ("Happy Birthday, Ludwig!") and some can be quite harmful, erasing data or causing your hard disk to require reformatting. A virus that replicates itself by resending itself as an e-mail attachment or as part of a network message is known as a worm.

Generally, there are three main classes of viruses:

File infectors. *Some file infector viruses attach themselves to program files, usually selected .COM or .EXE files. Some can infect any program for which execution is requested, including .SYS, .OVL, .PRG, and .MNU files. When the program is loaded, the virus is loaded as well. Other file infector viruses arrive as wholly-contained programs or scripts sent as an attachment to an e-mail note.*

System or boot-record infectors. *These viruses infect executable code found in certain system areas on a disk. They attach to the DOS boot sector on diskettes or the Master Boot Record on hard disks. A typical scenario (familiar to the author) is to receive a diskette from an innocent source that contains a boot disk virus. When your operating system is running, files on the diskette can be read without triggering the boot disk virus. However, if you leave the diskette in the drive, and then turn the computer off or reload the operating system, the computer will look first in your A drive, find the* *diskette with its boot disk virus, load it, and make it temporarily impossible to use your hard disk. (Allow several days for recovery.) This is why you should make sure you have a bootable floppy.*

Macro viruses. *These are among the most common viruses, and they tend to do the least damage. Macro viruses infect your Microsoft Word application and typically insert unwanted words or phrases.*

The computer virus, of course, gets its name from the biological virus. The word itself comes from a Latin word meaning slimy liquid or poison.

Mouse Trapping

 You might have been victim to mouse trapping if you have been to a website and then tried to go to another and it would not let you leave. It would just keep opening the page you were just on, or when you try and close the browser another one opens up. It is a real pain and can jam up your system and may force you to reboot it.

Here is the whatis.com definition of Mouse Trapping:

This is a technique that forces a user to remain on a specific Web site opening more windows to that site when closing the original. Whenever the user tries to leave the site by closing the browser window or going to a new URL, the site that is mousetrapping will automatically open a new browser window with its URL or not allow the browser to go to the new URL. Some mousetraps will only open a limited number of new browser windows and eventually will let the persevering user leave the site; other mousetraps will open new browser windows ad infinitum, and the only way to get out of the trap is to press "Ctrl+Alt+Del" to end the task or reboot the computer if that fails.

Spyware

Spyware is a computer program that gathers information about a user without their knowledge. This information is used by companies and they in turn send it to advertisers and  other parties who may be interested. They can gather information such as personal (name, address, and phone number), software applications you have already installed on your computer, websites you have visited and the information you provided to those sites, if you clicked any banner advertisements, files you have downloaded and your ISP details. This is all sitting in the background of your computer and you have no knowledge of it's existence unless you scan your computer with a spyware detection program which can be found on the Internet for sale or for free.

Here is the whatis.com definition of spyware:

Spyware is any technology that aids in gathering information about a person or organization without their knowledge. On the Internet (where it is sometimes called a spybot or tracking software), spyware is programming that is put in someone's computer to secretly gather information about the user and relay it to advertisers or other interested parties. Spyware can get in a computer as a software virus or as the result of installing a new program.

Data collecting programs that are installed with the user's knowledge are not, properly speaking, spyware, if the user fully understands what data is being collected and with whom it is being shared. However, spyware is often installed without the user's consent, as a drive-by download, or as the result of clicking some option in a deceptive pop-up window. Software designed to serve advertising, known as adware, can usually be thought of as spyware as well because it almost invariably includes components for tracking and reporting user information. However, marketing firms object to having their products called "spyware." As a result, McAfee (the Internet security company) and others now refer to such applications as "potentially unwanted programs" (PUP).

The cookie is a well-known mechanism for storing information about an Internet user on their own computer. If a Web site stores information about you in a cookie that you don't know about, the cookie can be considered a form of spyware. Spyware is part of an overall public concern about privacy on the Internet.

Adware

The difference between adware and spyware to me is simple. With adware you know it is on your system, spyware you don't. Adware is similar in that it installs itself onto your computer, but advises you that it is gathering and using this type of information for advertising, marketing and other commercial purposes. Adware usually targets you with pop-up advertising based on your Internet browsing habits, but spyware records personal information.

BonziBuddy is an example of adware that is used by children. It is a talking purple gorilla that helps you navigate the Internet, sends e-mails and tells jokes. The odd banana is eaten as well. You knowingly install this application but if you read the fine print you will see that it collects information and shares it with consultants and affiliates for internal business purposes.

Here is the whatis.com definition of adware:

Generically, adware (spelled all lower case) is any software application in which advertising banners are displayed while the program is running. The authors of these applications include additional code that delivers the ads, which can be viewed through pop-up windows or through a bar that appears on a computer screen. The justification for adware is that it helps recover programming development cost and helps to hold down the cost for the user.

Adware has been criticized because it usually includes code that tracks a user's personal information and passes it on to third parties, without the user's authorization or knowledge. This practice has been dubbed spyware and has prompted an outcry from computer security and privacy advocates, including the Electronic Privacy Information Center.

Noted privacy software expert Steve Gibson of Gibson Research explains: "Spyware is any software (that) employs a user's Internet connection in the background (the so-called 'backchannel') without their knowledge or explicit permission. Silent background use of an Internet 'backchannel' connection must be preceded by a complete and truthful disclosure of proposed backchannel usage, followed by the receipt of explicit, informed consent for such use. Any software communicating across the Internet absent of these elements is guilty of information theft and is properly and rightfully termed: Spyware."

A number of software applications, including Ad-Aware and OptOut (by Gibson's company), are available as freeware to help computer users search for and remove suspected spyware programs.

Phishing

Phishing is on the increase and it is a way for the bad guys to get our personal information easily. Phishing is an Internet term meaning "fishing for information". It is a way for the bad guy to get account information from your bank records to your e-bay account.

I get a lot of e-mails that appear to be from my bank site asking me to log in and put in my personal information. When you click on the link provided it looks just like your bank site, but don't be fooled – it isn't. They design these sites to look identical to your bank site (or other payment site like paypal or e-bay site etc.) so when you get there you feel comfortable in giving your information but what they will do is take your pin number and password and use them to go to the real site and take your money.

I just got one today that requested I log into my paypal account because someone was trying to access it. The funny thing is I don't have a paypal account. When I clicked the link I went to a site that was identical to the paypal site but I traced back it's origin and it was hosted overseas somewhere. If I did have an account and logged in they would have all my information and I am sure drain my account.

Never log into any website from an e-mail if you are not 100% sure it came from the advertised sender; you could be asking for a lot of trouble. No financial institution will request you to log in for security purpose. Please report any of these e-mails to your financial institution as well as I am sure they would want to know, and will probably do a security alert on their website.

Here is the whatis.com definition of phishing:

Phishing is e-mail fraud where the perpetrator sends out legitimate-looking e-mails that appear to come from well-known and trustworthy Web sites in an attempt to gather personal and financial information from the recipient. A phishing expedition, like the fishing expedition it's named for, is a speculative venture: the phisher puts the lure hoping to fool at least a few of the prey that encounter the bait. Web sites that are frequently spoofed by phishers include PayPal, eBay, MSN, Yahoo, BestBuy, and America Online.

Phishers use a number of different social engineering and e-mail spoofing ploys to try to trick their victims. In one fairly typical case before the Federal Trade Commission (FTC), a 17-year-old male sent out messages purporting to be from America Online that said there had been a billing problem with recipients' AOL accounts. The perpetrator's e-mail used AOL logos and contained legitimate links. If recipients clicked on the "AOL Billing Center" link, however, they were taken to a spoofed AOL Web page that asked for personal information, including credit card numbers, personal identification numbers (PINs), social security numbers, banking numbers, and passwords. This information was used for identity theft.

The FTC warns users to be suspicious of any official-looking e-mail message that asks for updates on personal or financial information and urges recipients to go directly to the organization's Web site to find out whether the request is legitimate. If you suspect you have been phished, forward the e-mail to uce@ftc.gov or call the FTC help line, 1-877-FTC-HELP

Chapter Seven

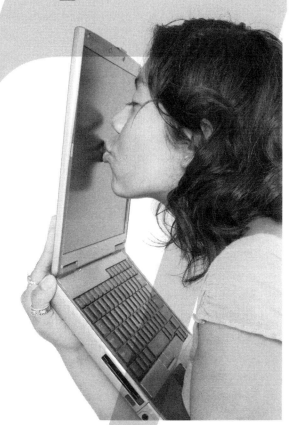

What are YOUR Kids Doing?

"Children seldom misquote you. In fact, they usually repeat word for word what you shouldn't have said."

Anonymous

Chapter 7

What are YOUR kids doing?

Tracking their Internet use.

After many of my presentations parents approach me and ask, "How do I know where my kids have been and what they are saying to others?" so I decided to add a chapter in this book on how to see where your children have been online, and how to log what and to who they have been speaking.

Some people feel this is an invasion of privacy and it is not the right thing for a parent to do. I believe as a parent, what happens under my roof is all fair to make sure our  children are safe. If that means looking at the Internet history and reviewing chat logs, then I will do it. I will leave it up to you whether you use these or not, but for those who want to take a peek then I will go over in this chapter how to view the Internet history files and how to activate the logging features on some of the chat programs I spoke about previously.

Keep in mind that children know a lot about how Internet history files work and how to deactivate the logging features on the chat programs. They can delete the history files on the computer but it is worth giving you this information if it stops one child from being harmed.

We will start with the history files using Internet Explorer (the most popular web browser) and for this I can include screen captures to walk you through the process. For other web browsers I will simply walk you through using text.

 ## Internet Explorer

Open your Internet Explorer application

There are 2 ways to check the history in Internet Explorer. The first way is go to through the "Tools" option in Internet Explorer as follows:

Viewing Internet Explorer History Files
(Option #1)

Once Internet Explorer starts go to the toolbar on the top and click on "**Tools**" then choose "**Internet Options**"

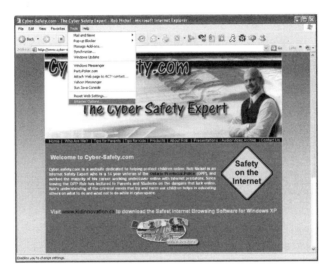

Click the "**General**" tab at the top of the box and you will see a section called "**Temporary Internet Files**"; Click on "**Settings**"

Under "**Settings…**" you will see all the options for logging your history files. To see where users of your computer have been you can click on the "**View Files…**" button.

Here you will see all the information about where users of your computer have been on the Internet. If you see a file or web address that looks suspicious or questionable you can click on it.

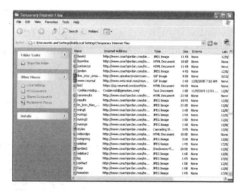

When you click on this location you will get a message asking: "Running a system command on this item might be unsafe. Do you wish to continue?". You can click on '**YES**' to show the content of the site.

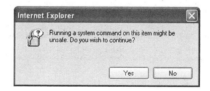

Clicking on these files will bring them up in Internet Explorer as the website itself or the image from that site. If you see a site or image with the label "xxx" or "porn" you may want to take a look. If you want to find out when this page or image was last accessed (or viewed) you will have to either scroll to the left on the history view page or maximize the window to see more information.

Note: Not all sites that are logged in temporary Internet files have shown on the computer. It may be because of a popup momentarily, or because of a hidden link to a website, however if this site is in there numerous times, this link appears or images, this should raise some suspicion and your child should be asked about visiting these sites.

Viewing Internet Explorer History Files – Option #2

The second way to view the history file in Internet Explorer is to open your Internet Explorer application like step 1 in the above but then instead of opening "**Tools**" you go to the "**View**" option and click on the "**History**" option.

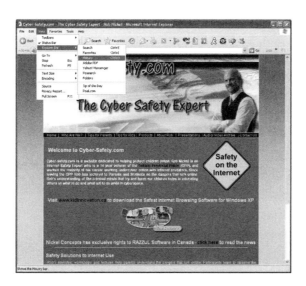

119

You will then see a menu bar appear on the left hand side of your screen. It will give you options to view the current day, the day before or weeks previous, so choose when you would like to view.

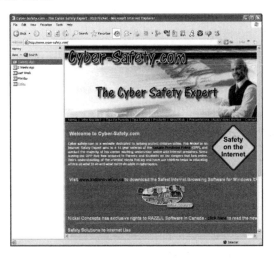

Once you choose the time frame you would like to view it will show folders showing the websites the people using that computer have viewed. When you click on those folders each page that was viewed will appear and you can then click on those sites to see the content of those pages on the right hand side of the browser window.

You can use the left hand bar to view these pages and go back and choose others.

This is probably the easiest way to view the history file, however you can only see what time frame it was visited – to get the exact time and date the site was accessed, use the other sequence to view the history files. The time and date will show.

 ## Netscape Navigator

In Netscape 7.0, open the application, and on the top toolbar click on the "**Go**" button and click "**History**".

You can then scroll down the list to see the sites that have been accessed by people using this application. To check the content of this site, just double click on that site, you then double click again on the web site that appears below it.

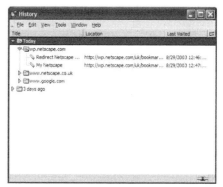

121

In **Netscape 8.0** open the application and on the top toolbar click on the **"Go"** button and click **"History"**. You can then scroll down the list on the left side to see the sites that have been accessed by people using this application. To view the sites, click on the date or web site, then click the web site that appears below that word and the content of the web site will show.

Safari 1.x for Macintosh

Open the Safari application by clicking the icon in the Dock. Then select the **"History"** menu from the menu bar. Choose the date you wish to review and a submenu will show up showing a list of sites for that particular date. Select the site that is listed in the submenu.

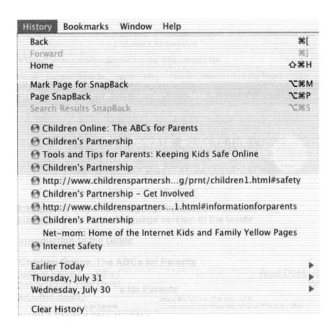

Logging Instant Messaging Chats

Knowing what your children view on Internet sites is one thing, but reading their chat logs is another. Again this is up to you whether you do this or not but I thought I would include in this book how you can log files in different chat applications or view them if they are already enabled.

The only way to activate the logging or archiving is to have the user logged onto the program, so these steps are used if your child left the computer on and he/she is still logged onto the chat program. There are programs out there that you can download or purchase (some are free of charge) that you can install and they will allow you to activate the logging features and then view them without the child knowing, but I cannot recommend them because I have not tested them and I do not know exactly how they work. If you search for MSN chat logs through a search engine you will find companies who specialize in these types of programs.

 The following are instructions on how to activate the logging feature on **MSN Messenger**:

With the MSN messenger program open, click on the "**Tools**" button and select "**Options**". This will take you to all of the options within this program. Click on the "**Messages**" button on the left hand side and you will see message history. This is where you check the box that says "**Automatically keep a history of my conversations**" and you can set the location on your hard drive to store all of the chat logs. This is also the location where you can find these files in the future just using Windows Explorer feature.

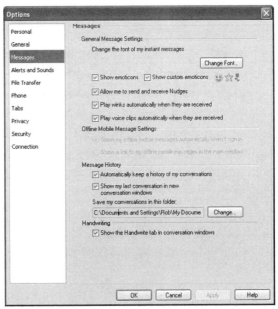

Your MSN is now saving all conversations into a log file on your computer's hard drive.

There are 2 ways to access these files. The first is to have MSN open and connected to the service and going through the following steps.

Click on the **"File"** button at the top and choose the **"View Message History"** button.

You will then see the following screen which will show you all the people on your child's list of friends.

When you choose one of these individuals you will then see the chats between your child and them.

If MSN Messenger is not open you can go to your Windows Explorer by right clicking on the start button and choosing the "**Explore**" option in the menu.

You will then see your hard drive contents and you will then go to the location where the logging was set in the steps above on how to activate the logging. The default location is under the "**My Documents/My Received Files/**" and under that directory you will see usernames with a numeric code. Click that folder and you will see a file folder called "**History**". You will then see files that are called XML files. Right click on those and choose "**Open with**" and pick your web browser (in this example it is

Internet Explorer). If it does not show, go to "**Choose Program**" and select from there.

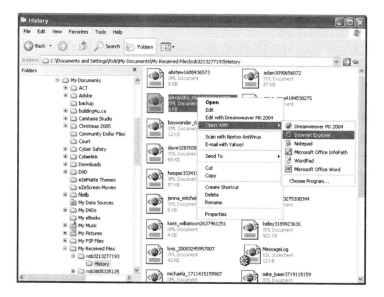

Then the log will show the following:

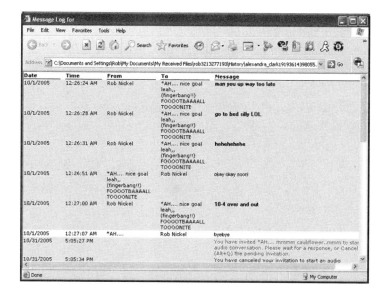

The following are instructions on how to activate the logging feature on **Yahoo Messenger**:

First step is to click on the "**Messenger**" button on the top. Then choose the "**Preferences**" button to access options for Yahoo Messenger.

Then go to the "**Archive**" button on the left and check the box that says "**Enable Archiving**". This will start logging all conversations in any chats from that point on. If this box is already checked then there are already logs on your computer.

There are two ways to check the logs for Yahoo Messenger on your system.

The first is to access them using Yahoo Messenger while it is open and logged onto your child's account. Click on the "**Contacts**" tab at the top of the application, and then "**Message Archive**" button.

You will see a box appear and on the left hand side are the people there are logs for and on the right top a date, a person's name and your child's profile name. If you click on the "**Messages**" folder on the left side of the screen, all messages will appear on the upper right side of the screen according to date. If you click on one of these dates the chat conversation will appear on the bottom right. You can also click on just the person's folder on the left hand side to see all conversations with that person. From there you can view all chat conversations.

What are they saying?

The other question I am asked after a presentation is, "What language are they speaking? I read the screen sometimes and all I see are a bunch of letters that are supposed to mean something I guess. The one I see most is 'POS' – what the heck does that mean?".

Well the fact is "POS" means a few different things. The main one is "Parents Over Shoulder" so they have to watch what they say. I am including a list of the most frequently used acronyms children use, but I am including a full list on the CD attached to the back cover of this book so parents can use it as an electronic reference.

Here are the main ones you need to know, to get used to speaking Internet.

Acronym	What It Means
A3	Anytime, anywhere, anyplace
AAMOF	As a matter of fact
ADN	Any day now
AFAIK	As far as I know
AFK	Away from keyboard
AKA	Also known as
AS	Another subject
ASL	Age, sex, location
ASLP	Age, sex, location, picture
ASAP	As soon as possible
ATB	All the best
ATK	At the keyboard
ATM	At the moment
AWA	As well as
B	Be
B4	Before
BAK	Back at keyboard
BBIAB	Be back in a bit
B/C	Because
BC	Be Cool
BCNU	Be seeing you
BBFN	Bye bye for now

Acronym	What It Means
BBL	Be back later
BBS	Be back soon
BD	Big Deal
BF	Boyfriend
BFN	Bye for now
BFZ4EVR	Best friends forever
BHL8	Be home late
BIF	Before I forget
BL	Belly laughing
BN	Been
BOL	Best of luck
BOT	Back on topic
BRB	Be right back
BRH	Be right here
BRBGP	Be right back gotta pee
BRT	Be right there
BTDT	Been there, done that
BTOBD	Be there or be dead
BTW	By the way
B4N	Before now
C	See
CU	See you
CU2	See you too
CUBL8R	Call you back later
CU@	See you at
CYA	See you around – or – See You
CMI	Call me
CMON	Come on
CTN	Can't talk now
CUL8R	See you later
CYO	See you online
DK	Don't know

Acronym	What It Means
DNR	Dinner
EG	Evil grin
EOD	End of discussion
EOS	End of story
EZ	Easy
F	Female
F?	Are we friends
F2F	Face to face
F2T	Free to talk
FAQ	Frequently asked questions
FC	Fingers crossed
FCOL	For crying out loud
FOFL	Falling on the floor laughing
FITB	Fill in the blank
FOAF	Friend of a friend
FS	For sale
FTF	Face to face
FUBAR	F__ked up beyond all recognition
FWIW	For what it's worth
FYEO	For your eyes only
FYA	For your amusement
GA	Go ahead
GAC	Get a clue
GAL	Get a life
GDW	Grin, duck, and weave
GF	Girlfriend
GG	Good game
GJ	Good job
GL	Good luck
GMTA	Great minds think alike
GOL	Giggling out loud
GR8	Great

Acronym	What It Means
GTG	Got to go
H	Hug
HB	Hug back
H8	Hate
HAGN	Have a good night
HH	Haha
HOAS	Hold on a second
HRU	How are you
HSIK	How should I know
HT4U	Hot for you
HTH	Hope that helps
H&K	Hugs and kisses
IAC	In any case
IAD8	It's a date
IC	I see
IDK	I don't know
IIRC	If I recall correctly
ILU	I love you
ILU2	I love you too
ILY	I love you
IMO	In my opinion
IMHO	In my humble opinion
IMNSHO	In my not so humble opinion
IOW	In other words
IRL	In real life
ITILY	I think I love you
IUSS	If you say so
IYD	In your dream
IYKWIM	If you know what I mean
JAM	Just a minute
JAS	Just a second
J4F or JFF	Just for fun

Acronym	What It Means
J4K or JFK	Just for kicks
JK	Just kidding
JMO	Just my opinion
K	Okay
KC	Keep cool
KHUF	Know how you feel
KISS	Keep it simple stupid
KIT	Keep in touch
KOTC	Kiss on the cheek
KOTL	Kiss on the lips
KWIM	Know what I mean
L8	Late
L8R	Later
LDR	Long distance relationship
LJBF	Let's just be friends
LMAO	Laughing my ass off
LOL	Laugh out loud
LTNS	Long time no see
LULAS	I love you like a sister
LUM	Love you man
LUV	Love
LY	Love you
LYN	Lying
M8	Mate
M	Male
MOB	Mobile
MOTD	Message of the day
MMA	Meet me at
MMAMP	Meet me at my place
MU	Miss you
MUSM	Miss you so much
MTE	My thoughts exactly

Acronym	What It Means
MYOB	Mind your own business
NA	No access
NBD	No big deal
NRN	No reply necessary
NC	No comment or Not cool
NE	Any
NE1	Anyone
NITING	Anything
NM	Not much
NP	No problem
NQA	No questions asked
NW	No way
NWO	No way out
OTFL	On the floor laughing
OIC	Oh, I see
OMG	Oh my God
OT	Off topic
OTOH	On the other hand
O4U	Only for you
P911	My parents are coming
PITA	Pain in the ass
PCM	Please call me
PLS	Please
PLZ	Please
PPL	People
POS	Parents over shoulder or Piece of sh*t
PRT	Party
PRW	Parents are watching
QT	Cutie
R	Are
RL	Real life
RLR	Earlier

Acronym	What It Means
RMB	Ring my bell
ROFL	Rolling on the floor laughing
ROTFLMAO	Rolling on the floor laughing my ass off
ROTG	Rolling on the ground
RS	Real soon
RSN	Real soon now
RTFM	Read the flaming manual
RU	Are you
RUMF?	Are you male or female
RUOK	Are you okay
S	Smile
SA	Sibling alert
SC	Stay cool
SEC	Wait a second
SK8	Skate
SOHF	Sense of humour failure
SOL	Smiling out loud
SOS	Same old stuff
SLM	See last mail
SLY	Still love you
SPK	Speak
SRY	Sorry
STATS	Your sex and age
SWALK	Sent with a loving kiss
SYS	See you soon
TA	Teacher alert
TBC	To be continued
TBYB	Try before you buy
TC	Take care
TCOY	Take care of yourself
THX	Thanks
TIA	Thanks in advance

Acronym	What It Means
TMI	Too much information
TMIY	Take me I'm yours
THNQ	Thank you
TNX	Thanks
TOY	Thinking of you
TTFN	Ta ta for now
TTYL	Talk to you later
TUL	Tell you later
TWF	That was fun
TY	Thank you
U2	You too
U	You
UR	You are
U4E	Yours forever
W8	Wait
W/	With
WB	Welcome back or Write back
W/E	Whatever
W/O	Without
WOT	What
WRT	With respect to
WRU	Where are you
WT	Without thinking
WTF	What the f__k
WTH	What the hell
WTG	Way to go
WUF	Where are you from
WUWH	Wish you were here
W4U	Waiting for you
X	Kiss
XO	Kisses and hugs
XLNT	Excellent

Acronym	What It Means
Y	Why
YGBSM	You have got to be kidding me
YGM	You got mail
YIU	Yes I understand
YIWTGP	Yes I want to go private
YR	You are
YSWUS	Yeah sure whatever you say
YW	You're welcome
ZZZ	Sleeping
?	Huh
?4U	Question for you
1ON1	One on one
2L8	Too late
2MORO	Tomorrow
2NITE	Tonight
3 8 1	Three words, eight letters, one meaning – I love you
4	For
4GM	Forgive me
4GVN	Forgiven
4YEO	For your eyes only
8	Ate

Chapter Eight

The Cyber-Bully

"If we are to teach real peace in this world, and if we are to carry on a real war against war, we shall have to begin with the children."

Mohandas Karamchand Gandhi

Chapter 8

The Cyber-Bully

Any day of the week you can turn on the Dr. Phil Show, Oprah, or any other talk show and you will find they are discussing bullying. This topic has become a big topic because there is such an increase in not only the schoolyard bullying, but now it has turned into the electronic world as well. Bullies can now post things about people that hurt, and it doesn't just stay in the schoolyard. It is there for the world to see.

The anonymity of the Internet has allowed children to feel a little more at ease at being the "Tough Guy". It is like in the old days before call display. Making those prank phone calls because there was no way to find out who was calling.

Although the typical bully is someone in the schoolyard everyone knows and fears, today the online bully can be much more intimidating and damaging to our youth. The children of today have an interactive world away from supervision. Most children spend their time online alone, with no adult supervision, which gives them the opportunity to get into trouble. Bullies tend to do their work away from adults so the Internet is the perfect place to reach others, anytime, anyplace while staying somewhat anonymous. That means that the victims are not even safe in their own home anymore. The place where they used to

143

be able to escape from bullies has now been lost with the wired world.

There are many ways bullies can reach their victims online. E-mails or instant messaging is obviously the favourite way to send threats or insults. They can also post messages on schoolmate's blog sites or guest books. Kids seem to share their passwords to e-mail accounts with their friends and in the hands of a bully that can be very dangerous. Children should never share their passwords to anything with anybody. There have been cases where bullies have created a whole website to target individuals who they feel the need to intimidate.

There have been cases where camera-enabled cell phones have been used to take pictures of students in the shower, and then posted on a website or distributed through e-mail, as well as posted on blog sites, and web pages. The Internet does make it hard to tackle the bully problem because when these incidents happen at school the teachers can be made aware of it and do something about it, but the Cyber-bully makes it difficult to detect in schools and it is not the jurisdiction of the school any longer.

I mentioned earlier in the book how people can intimidate using online chats combined with using Trojan programs to hack into someone's computer and make them do things in fear. Fear of getting in trouble with their parents or others, and this is just another way bullies can manipulate and make a child's life miserable.

What are the laws in regards to online bullying? In Canada, is there an offence in the Criminal Code for such a thing? Well, it all depends on the case but the youth in Canada should be aware that some forms of online bullying are considered to be criminal acts.

The Criminal Code of Canada states that it is a crime to communicate repeatedly with someone if your communication causes them to fear for their own safety or the safety of others.

Online Bullies may be violating the Canadian Human Rights Act, if they spread hate or discrimination based on race, national or ethnic origin, colour, religion, age, sex, sexual orientation, marital status, family status or disability.

It would also be a crime to publish a "defamatory libel" or to write something that is designed to insult a person or likely to injure a person's reputation by exposing him or her to hatred, contempt or ridicule.

Signs that your child may be a victim of a cyber-bully would be their reluctant use of the Internet all of a sudden. Your child may also be reluctant to attend school, faking sick or getting very anxious and nervous before leaving for school. Keep an eye on these signs, and then open the communication with your child to find out what the problem really is.

So what should the parent do? What action should we take in these types of situations? Easy answer – **Get Involved!**

The best way to combat cyber-bullies is to prevent bullying before it happens, and we do this by getting involved and educating our children. We should learn everything we can about the Internet (which is why you are reading this book – good for you) and talk to them about what they are doing online. What sites they visit and what they use the Internet for most. Find out what sites they are going to and who they are talking to, and do they have their own personal websites up for all to see.

We also have to let our children know that they can come to us anytime and talk to us if there was something that made them feel uncomfortable or threatening that they viewed online. When our children come to us with these concerns it is extremely important not to get upset or excited when they tell us these things; that is the way to make sure they never talk about it to us again.

We should also make sure our children understand the rules to Internet use. They have to be responsible when online by not posting or saying anything to others on the net that they would not want others to say to them. Make sure they understand that everything they say or post is up there for the whole world to see (including you as a parent).

I really suggest an online agreement that is signed by you and your child. I have included one in the CD attached to this book, for you to print out and sign with your child, with the basic rules for Internet use. This is very similar to the agreement I had with my parents about drinking and driving when I was a teen. Research has shown that in homes where parents have clear rules against certain kinds of activities, young people are much less likely to engage in them. So do up a contract with your children on responsible Internet use.

If you find your child is being bullied online you have to take action! If it is a schoolmate you should meet with school officials to meet the problem head-on and make the school aware there is a problem. Watch for the signs of bullying, and report any incident of online harassment and physical threats to your local police agency.

You should also go over all of the safety rules with your children to decrease the chance of anyone online finding out information about them. I cover these rules in the next chapter of this book. If your children are being harassed online you should make sure that they tell an adult about it, whether it is a teacher, parent, older sibling or relative. Tell them if they are ever being harassed online to leave the area that the bullying is taking place in and if it is taking place with an instant message program they should block that person from their list.

Blocking the Bully in Chat Programs

To block people on your **MSN Messenger** do the following:

Right click on the individual on your list that is causing you problems and choose the "**Block**" option.

You will then see a block sign by that MSN client meaning they will not see you when you are online. You can unblock this individual by doing the same thing but this time it will say "**unblock**" instead of block.

To block people on your **Yahoo Messenger** do the following:

Click the "**Messenger**" menu in Messenger and select "**Preferences**".

Click the "**Ignore List**" category.

Select the option labeled "**Ignore only the people below**".

Click the "**Add**" button.

Enter the Yahoo ID of the contact you wish to ignore.

Click the "**Ignore**" button.

Click "**OK**" at the bottom of the window.

You can ignore 100 contacts.

To block people on your **AOL Messenger** do the following:

Right click on the individual on your list that is causing you problems and choose the **"Block"** option.

This person is now blocked, meaning they will not see you when you are online. You can unblock this individual by doing the same thing but this time it will say **"unblock"** instead of block.

To block people on your **ICQ** List do the following:

Click on the "**Main Menu**" tab of the application.

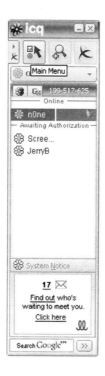

Click on the "**Preferences and Security**" tab.

Go to the "**Ignore list**" button and then click "**Add to Ignore List**"

Enter the person's ICQ number you wish to ignore (will be in the users information) then hit search – select the person and hit the "**Add**" button.

The user will then be added to the list and will not be able to see when you are online – or send communication to you.

Blocking Unwanted E-mails

If the bullying is through e-mails, you should block the sender in your e-mail program and save any messages and forward them to your ISP (Internet Service Provider). Most providers have an appropriate use policy that restricts users from harassing others over the Internet.

To put a person on your blocked e-mail list using Microsoft Outlook, just right click on the e-mail you received from this person and choose the junk e-mail option and pick **"Add sender to blocked e-mail list"** and this will stop all incoming e-mails from that person. Most e-mail programs have this feature in them and it is easy to locate by going to the help file of the program and searching for **"block e-mail"** and it should walk you through how to do it.

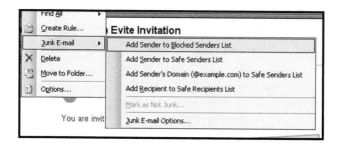

Remember bullying is everyone's problem and we all have to take steps to make sure our children feel safe in this world as well as the online world. Let's do our part to make sure they stay safe by staying informed and talking with our children about these issues.

Chapter Nine

Reducing
the Risks

"The best inheritance a parent can give to his children is a few minutes of their time each day."

M. Grundler

Chapter 9

Reducing the Risks

Household Rules

The first step in reducing risks online is talking. Talking to your children about what they should and should not do when they are online. Find out the activities they are currently doing online and talk about them. Children love to show off their talents, and when you are interested in what they are doing online, nine times out of ten they will be more than happy to show you what they know. Let them teach you some of the different chat programs they use, what sites they visit and music download software they use.

The next step is to let them know the rules in the house to online use. An Internet use contract is on the CD included with this book; you and your children can read it and sign it so there are no misunderstandings of appropriate use in your home.

I will now cover the rules of online safety so you have a good understanding of how to keep your children safe in a wired world.

1. Make sure your child does not spend all of his/her time on the computer. People, not computers, should be their best friends and companions.

This is a rule that has recently been enforced at our house. I use RAZZUL software at home and it is great for children, but because of all the games that can be accessed online for kids, it seems my girls are getting a little addicted to it. I have also activated the time limit feature in the software to only allow a certain amount of time online on weekends and weekdays. There is no time allowed on the Internet until all homework is completed and chores done as well. This rule is important especially in this day and age when childhood obesity is on the increase due to lack of exercise. I would much rather see my children having fun outside with their friends, than inside watching TV or in front of a computer.

Too many parents use the Internet as a babysitter, much like the TV. When we have things to do it is nice to have our children occupied, but let's make sure they are not spending all of their time glued to the computer screen.

2. Keep the computer in an area where it can be monitored, like the family room, kitchen or living room, not in your child's bedroom.

I am always surprised during my lectures at how many parents have a computer in their child's bedroom connected to the Internet. Computers hooked to the

Internet should always be in an area where it can be monitored by adults. My wife and I built a home 3 years ago and when designing it we made sure there was a desk area between the kitchen and the family room for a computer to sit. This is where my children can access the Internet and it is always in view of us whether we are in the kitchen or family room. We had the luxury or designing our house to accommodate this but no matter how your home is set up it is always possible to put the computer area in a place where it can be monitored, especially in this day of wireless networks in our homes.

Other homes have the computer in the basement, but I have to ask - is that a place where parents frequent? Usually not, and it is not a great place to have the computer hooked to the Internet either. We have to be able to see what our children are doing online. We have to monitor activity to make sure they are staying safe.

3. Learn enough about computers so you can enjoy them together with your kids.

You have read this book so now you are learning! Again I suggest you sit down with your children and let them teach you more. You will be surprised at how eager they  will be to show you their abilities. We all like to brag a bit and children are no different.

If you have to search for something for work or find an interest or hobby on the Internet, ask your kids to help.

Have them show you the best way to search for things and locate them. Spend some quality time with them, and let them teach you.

4. Teach them never to meet an online friend offline unless you are with them.

Although this sounds like common sense, so many children have met with people in person that they met online as a stranger. I explained how easy it is to build rapport with children, but unfortunately children don't really understand this concept. Children are very trusting and don't think there are people in this world who will harm them. It is up to you to let them know they do exist. There are too many children who have gone missing because of these types of meetings. We see them in the news every week. If there is one rule in this whole book you remember, remember this one; children should never, I repeat NEVER meet with someone in person they have met online unless accompanied by a parent, not another older friend, **A PARENT!**

5. Watch your children when they're online and see where they go.

Now that your computer is out in the open (Rule Number 2) keep an eye on what sites they like to visit, or what chat programs they like to use. Knowing what your children are doing online will help you determine how much time they should be spending online as well as give you an idea of why they use the Internet. You may see them going to sites that are not really appropriate for them and when you see this you can now discuss this with them, and advise them why it is not appropriate. You can also see how many people are on their chat list, or what chat rooms they are going into and what the topic of that room is. Remember, POS means "Parents over shoulder!"

6. Make sure that your children feel comfortable coming to you with questions and don't over react if things go wrong.

Communication is the key and your children have to know that they can come to you with any problems and not get the third degree. I explained a past investigation in this book

where the young girl did not want to get into trouble for having a virus on the computer so she complied with a boy's request to take naked pictures of herself. This is a perfect example of being afraid of going to your parents with a problem, and I don't have to tell you how much worse that outcome was. Sit down with your children and let them know they can come to you with any problem that arises from not only their Internet use, but any problems they encounter in life.

7. Keep kids out of chatrooms or IRC channels unless they are monitored.

This sounds like a definite rule and to a certain extent it is. I am not a big fan of chatrooms because of all the nonsense that occurs within them. I have entered teen chatrooms during investigations to find that children can use foul language and they use these arenas to spout off (flame) and bully others. I don't feel they are a healthy place for children to hang out, but if your child feels they just have to be in them, then they should be monitored at all times. Links to inappropriate sites are posted in these rooms and in the IRC (Internet Relay Chat) channels, files are traded to occupants that are not only inappropriate but illegal as well. There are certain websites that have monitored chatrooms for children but again these should be approved by the parents. Instant messaging with friends is common for most youth, but the need for chatrooms where many unknown individuals hang out is not a necessity.

8. Encourage discussions between you and your child about what they enjoy online.

Again keeping that line of communication open with your children about their likes and dislikes on the net enhances online activity for the child, and gives you some peace of mind as the parent.

9. Teach them what information they can share with others online and what they can't (like telephone numbers, address, their full name and school)

No information about your child should be given out over the Internet no matter what. I know that as children get older they will want to do things like having a blog site where they can do a daily journal but for the very young, absolutely no information should be given out whatsoever. Giving out this information is just giving ammunition to predators. Just a name could be enough to gather information about your child, not to mention what school they go to, phone number and address. Let your children know that this is one rule that must be abided by no matter what.

10. Get to know their "online friends" just as you get to know all of their other friends.

Just like we like to know who our children are hanging out with at school, we should know who they are chatting with online. Have your child explain who these friends are, where they met them and why they like talking with them. Signs that they may be speaking to people they should not would be a sudden shutdown of the computer when you walk by, or switching screens on the computer. You might also note if your children are getting phone calls from people you don't know or they are getting gifts from people you do not know in the mail. This is a very common occurrence with predators over the Internet.

11. Warn them that people may not be what they seem to be and that people they chat with are not their friends, they are just people they chat with.

Even though the majority of children on the net have pretended to be someone else, someone older or even a different sex, they seem to think everyone else tells the truth online. As a parent you have to drill into them that a

 lot of people pretend and are not who they say they are online, even if they know the lingo, or have sent a picture of themselves.

I recently received a call from an adult who had sent money overseas to have his girlfriend fly here to Canada to visit. She never arrived and had a story that she needed more money because they would not let her on the plane for a bunch of different reasons. My first response was, "sorry to say it but you have been taken". He said "but she sent me pictures of herself and everything." That was all it took; a picture to say "this is me" and he believed it. Now he is out a bunch of money all because someone pretended to be someone else. I found in most of my investigations, the majority of people you speak with online are not really who they say they are, especially in the younger chatrooms.

12. Discuss these rules, get your children to agree to adhere to them, and post them near the computer as a reminder.

 One thing I have learned as a motivational speaker is that posting things around my office helps me not only remember but to adhere to them. When I see affirmations every day, it keeps me on track and the same goes for rules. If they are discussed and posted, chances are your children will abide by them. Included in the CD in the back of this book is also the list of rules from this chapter. You can print them out and post them at your computer so everyone in your house knows the rules.

Rules for Children

1. I will never give out personal details that would identify who I am, such as my name, address, phone number, school or photographs.

2. I will tell a parent or teacher if I see any bad language or pictures on the Internet, or if anyone writes me anything I don't like.

3. I will not reply to any messages or bulletin board items that are suggestive, obscene, aggressive, or distressing.

4. I will not use bad language online, neither will I take part in arguments or fights online.

5. I will not accept any offers of money or presents, even free offers.

6. I will never order anything online or give out credit card details.

7. I will not enter chat rooms and websites that I have agreed with my parents are off-limits.

8. I will not arrange any face-to-face meetings with anyone I have met on the Internet unless my parents consent and they accompany me.

Chapter Ten

Software
to Help

"Kid Innovation Canada is a company committed to providing a safe online computing environment for children."

Kid Innovation Canada

Chapter 10

Software to Help

With 99% of our youth online in today's society, how can we help protect them without being behind their back watching every letter they type, and viewing every webpage they go to? Well, technology brought us the Internet and technology also brought us software applications that help to keep our children protected.

There are many different software applications on the market to help keep children safe online. You will hear the terms blocking software and filtering software, which aid in the protection of children, but I am going to explain the difference so you can make an informed decision on what you think is best for your home.

Blocking Software

Blocking software uses what is called a "black list" or bad site list. It does just as it says – it blocks bad sites from showing up on your computer. Some companies update this list regularly and it also lets you add sites you feel should be on the list as well. Some companies keep this list to themselves and don't allow users to change any

of the sites. The problem with this technology is that there are new sites every day and some could get through and show on your computer if the list is not updated frequently enough, or is not known for some time. With over 160,000 new websites registered every day you can imagine how tough it is to keep this list updated and the categories maintained.

Filtering Software

Filtering helps with and enhances blocking by scanning the site that is requested to be accessed and looks for keywords that are believed to be in a site that should be blocked. The filtering software that is a stand-alone application can have it's drawbacks, like filtering innocent sites because of words such as "sex", which is not always used in an inappropriate manner. For instance, you may want to search for "sextuplets" or "Essex County" and these sites would not appear because they would have been filtered out.

Some filtering software companies let you choose what to block out, and have keywords in a database that automatically look for those words in a site to filter them out. You may want to block pornography and drug sites, but can allow gaming sites. You may want to allow all but pornography sites; it would be totally up to you as the end user. Again, like blocking, this is not 100% accurate because some sites misspell words so filtering does not work, or it may just have images that filtering cannot scan (well not yet but I am sure technology will come soon that will assist in this as well.)

Outgoing Filtering

This is one of the coolest features in the filtering market, and one I highly recommend. It means that if a child tries to type in things such as phone number, his/her name or address and send them in an instant message or e-mail, the outgoing filtering software replaces these words with "xxxxxxx". As a parent, you set up what words should not go out into the wired world  and when the filtering software scans messages, e-mails or any content leaving your computer it will replace with "x's" so there will be no way for the bad guys to obtain this information.

When I first saw this technology, years ago, I thought it was probably the coolest thing going, and that all computers should have this technology built into them.

Even though our children know the rules and we are confident they will abide by them, there should be no doubt that our children's identity will remain a secret. So I give outgoing filtering a big thumbs up.

Monitoring and Tracking Software

This is usually the type of software parent's use for the older children in the house. They feel that when their children are old enough they should not be blocking and filtering but they still want to know that their children are not spending too much time online, and want to know just where they are spending all of their time.

Monitoring and tracking software does just what it says, monitors a child's activities online or tracks where they have been and what they are doing online. I have used this software myself, not so much for my children but for my babysitters. I installed this software and let them know that while they are online they should not be doing anything illegal or anything that would not be appropriate in my home. There are some applications that can run "in the background", meaning people on the computer have no idea that they are being monitored. Some parents are appalled that I would suggest spying on children, but my answer is always the same. It is my home, and my computer, I have a right to know what people are doing online using my Internet connection.

Firewall Software

A firewall can block different types of unwanted material from getting to your computer. It is basically a barrier or a filter at your Internet connection that can block certain materials or hackers from entering your computer system. The Whatis.com definition for a firewall is:

A firewall is a set of related programs, located at a network gateway server, that protects the resources of a private network from users from

172

other networks. (The term also implies the security policy that is used with the programs.) An enterprise with an intranet that allows its workers access to the wider Internet installs a firewall to prevent outsiders from accessing its own private data resources and for controlling what outside resources its own users have access to.

Basically, a firewall, working closely with a router program, examines each network packet to determine whether to forward it toward its destination. A firewall also includes or works with a proxy server that makes network requests on behalf of workstation users. A firewall is often installed in a specially designated computer separate from the rest of the network so that no incoming request can get directly at private network resources.

There are a number of firewall screening methods. A simple one is to screen requests to make sure they come from acceptable (previously identified) domain name and Internet Protocol addresses. For mobile users, firewalls allow remote access in to the private network by the use of secure logon procedures and authentication certificates.

A number of companies make firewall products. Features include logging and reporting, automatic alarms at given thresholds of attack, and a graphical user interface for controlling the firewall.

Computer security borrows this term from firefighting, where it originated. In firefighting, a firewall is a barrier established to prevent the spread of fire.

Anti-virus Software

Anti-virus software is software that I have on every computer in my home and in my opinion probably the most important to have on any system. New viruses are coming out every day, and most anti-virus software companies are on top of this and keep their virus list updated daily. It is one thing to have this software on your computer and another to make sure it is updated regularly. You must always have this software and make sure you update the list of current viruses and Trojans out there on the Internet.

We have all heard of someone who has been a victim of a virus and lost important documents in the process. Anti-virus software assists in making sure we do not become these victims.

I use Norton's Internet Security which is a software package that is a firewall, and anti-virus program in one. There is a list of different applications and sites in Chapter 11 of this book. Find the one that is right for you, and install it as soon as possible.

 by

Well I am sure you have already realized my pick for the best safety software on the Internet is RAZZUL. That is exactly why I got involved with the company in 2005. I had seen a lot of applications out there but instead of filtering and blocking, I thought the most effective way to protect was by the use of a "white list" application. In other words, just let access to child approved sites to be viewed by children, and that is exactly what Kid Innovation Inc. had accomplished. When I saw this I knew it was the company I wanted to be associated with. I love RAZZUL, my wife loves RAZZUL and more importantly, my kids love it too.

It not only just allows child-approved sites in but it also filters the sites as well as a double precaution. Some sites can change, and RAZZUL makes sure if they are different they will not have any inappropriate content on them.

Razzul unlocks the power of the Internet for children with its innovative approach to online safety and parental control. Containing features which allow them to use the  computer virtually unattended or with adults at their side, Razzul provides children freedom – and parent's peace of mind.

Web access is a snap and allows viewing of kid-friendly web sites that are perfect for any child. Plus, with its unique method of access to the Yahooligan's search engine, parents can rest assured their children won't miss out on any of the capabilities of the World Wide Web. Once they're logged in to Razzul, kids enter their own private ePlayground for online enjoyment that every parent can trust.

- Access to kid-friendly Web sites only – more than 25,000.

- Custom Windows XP Login – a personal login icon for children, allowing them to enjoy Razzul, the Internet and their e-mail, with or without adult assistance. At the same time Razzul completely locks out the child's ability to access any other programs or files.

- Web page content filtering – in addition to allowing access to kid-friendly sites only, Razzul goes one step further in assuring children's safety online. Each page is scanned for objectionable words, which are restricted from your child's view. Razzul comes with many language restrictions already built into its proprietary database, which can be customized by the parent.

- Access to pre-installed applications or games.

- Real-time parent override – at any time, parents can override a banned or restricted site, allowing their child immediate access so they may continue surfing uninterrupted.

- Instant e-mail access – Sending and receiving e-mail messages to and from parent-approved e-mail addresses is just one click away for kids. Simply click on the e-mail icon in the Razzul start menu to go immediately to the e-mail screens, giving children their own spam-free e-mail account!

- One-click access to favourites.

- Full browser functionality – children can navigate pages, print any web page, refresh the screen or return to their Razzul Home Page at any time.

- Easy access menus to preferred sites. Razzul Administration Features. By using the controls available at the Razzul Admin Web site, parents have complete access to many features to help track where their children go on the net, who they e-mail with, how adults get alerted and much more.

Parent Administration can be accessed anywhere from the web and is fast and easy. By logging in with an e-mail and password – and using the controls on the main admin web page – parents have one-click access to all of the administration features. They can update their child information, view online activity, configure e-mail settings, allow or block websites and words, modify schedules, create reminders and more at www.razzul.com/manage.

Schedule and Log

With Razzul, parents can schedule the amount of time their child surfs the web by limiting time access to the number of hours per day or by specific times throughout a day. And while children are online surfing or checking e-mail, parents can have pre-set reminders or motivational messages pop up for them to see.  Remind a child to clean his room or have a motivational message waiting for her when she gets home from school: "Good job on your test today!!!"

While adults are away, Razzul is not. The Razzul software will record all of a child's browsing activity. You can select a day and view all the web sites that have been visited and whether the sites were allowed or blocked. Customize the view to show all web sites, denied sites or allowed sites.

Pop-up and Ad Blocking

Pop-up ads, surveys and banners can be frustrating and confusing for a child. Razzul eliminates annoying pop-up ads and windows from being displayed. The Razzul method of eliminating the annoyance means children have a clean, easy-to-use screen at all times.

Child E-mail

Kids love e-mail. How about child@razzulcity.com? Razzul offers a custom e-mail account to be created for each child. Kids can only exchange e-mail with pre-approved addresses that parents set up in their address book. And every outgoing or incoming e-mail is scanned for the language restrictions defined within Razzul. The language restrictions can be customized to add words that adults would like to restrict a child from sending – perhaps a home phone number or address. Parents also have the ability to view any e-mail exchanged, even if the child deletes it from view. Parents can also release an e-mail that is held up for content, destined for an unauthorized recipient or received from an unauthorized sender coming in.

Alerts

Razzul Alerts can be set up to notify parents when a child attempts to access a forbidden web site, arrives at a web site containing inappropriate content, receives a restricted e-mail or attempts to send e-mail to an unauthorized recipient. Those alerts can be sent immediately or summarized at the end of each day.

Favourites

If children have favourite sites they like to visit frequently, parents can add them to their favourites list from within the Razzul administration site. From the favourites list in Razzul, a child can simply click on an identifiable name and immediately be directed to the site.

Skinnable Interface

Razzul offers a skinnable interface, so as new themes (or skins) become available, parents can choose which look they find the most acceptable for their child. The default skin is 'Razzul City' which offers a host of fun and educational sites.

Chapter Eleven

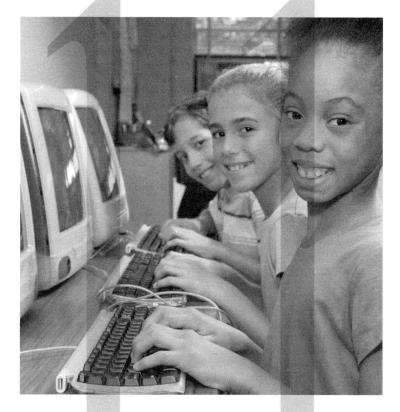

Online
Resources

"One generation plants the trees; another gets the shade."

Chinese Proverb

Chapter 11

Online Resources

Search Engines

Google	www.google.com
Yahoo! Search	www.search.yahoo.com
MSN Search	www.search.msn.com
AltaVista	www.altavista.com
Ask Jeeves	www.ask.com
Gigablast	www.gigablast.com
Netscape Search	www.netscape.com
Snap.com	www.snap.com
Teoma	www.teoma.com
Excite	www.excite.com

Internet Safety Sites

Cyber-Safety	www.cyber-safety.com
Get Net Wise	www.getnetwise.org

Net Smart	www.netsmartz.org
Safe Kids	www.safekids.com
Wired Safety	www.wiredsafety.org
Family Internet	www.familyinternet.about.com
Protect Kids.com	www.protectkids.com
Stay Safe Online	www.staysafeonline.com
Net Safe Kids	www.netsafekids.com
Web Aware	www.bewebaware.com
Cyber Tips	www.cybertips.ca

Filtering/Blocking Software Sites

Kid Innovation Canada	www.kidinnovation.ca
Cyber Patrol	www.cyberpatrol.com
CyberSITTER	www.cybersitter.com
Net Nanny	www.netnanny.com
Surf Control	www.surfcontrol.com
Content Protect	www.contentwatch.com
FilterPak	www.surfguardian.com
Cyber Sentinel	www.cybersentinel.com

McAfee Parental Controls	www.mcafee.com
Norton Parental Controls	www.symantec.com

Monitoring Software

Spector	www.spectorsoft.com
Spy Agent	www.spytech-web.com
IamBigBrother	www.iambigbrother.com
eBlaster	www.eblaster.com
Golden Eye	www.monitoring-spy-software.com
Guardian Monitor	www.guardiansoftware.com
Invisible Keylogger	www.invisiblekeylogger.com
007 Spy Software	www.e-spy-software.com
Spy Buddy	www.exploreanywhere.com
Key Logger Pro	www.exploreanywhere.com

Firewall Software

Norton Internet Security	www.symantec.com
Zone Alarm	www.zonealarm.com
Outpost Firewall Pro	www.agnitum.com

Norman Personal Firewall	www.norman.com
SurfSecret Personal Firewall	www.surfsecret.com
McAfee Personal Firewall Pro	www.mcafee.com
Bullguard	www.bullguard.com
Sygate Personal Firewall Pro	www.sygate.com
Injoy Firewall	www.fx.dk
BlackICE PC Protection	www.blackice.com

Anti-virus Software

Bit Defender	www.bitdefender.com
Kaspersky	www.kaspersky.com
F-Secure Anti-virus	www.f-secure.com
PC-cillin	www.trendmicro.com
ESET Nod32	www.nod32.com
McAfee VirusScan	www.mcafee.com
Norton AntiVirus	www.symantec.com
AVG AntiVirus	www..grisoft.com
eTrust EZ Antivirus	www.my-etrust.com
Norman Virus Control	www.normand.com

Spyware/Adware Software

Spy Sweeper	www.webroot.com
Aluria Anti-Spyware	www.aluriasoftware.com
CounterSpy	www.sunbelt-software.com
Trend Micro Anti-Spyware	www.trendmicro.com
AntiSpy	www.softvers.com
Spyware Doctor	www.pctools.com
PestPatrol	www.pestpatrol.com
Ad-aware Se/Pro	www.lavasoft.com
Spyware Be Gone	www.spywarebegone.com
McAfee Anti-Spyware	www.mcafee.com

Notes

Notes

Notes

If you have any comments or suggestions or you would like more information about Rob's services please use to following contact information:

Mail:

250 Dundas St. South, Unit #6
Cambridge, Ontario.
Canada
N1R 8A8

Phone: (519) 654-0002 Ext 1
Fax: (519)654-0002

E-mail:

rob@cyber-safety.com

Websites:

Cyber Safety Website
www.cyber-safety.com

Inspirational Speaking Website
www.rnickel.com

Nickel Concepts Website
www.nickelconcepts.com

Nickel Publishing Website
www.nickelpublishing.com

Kid Innovation Canada Website
www.kidinnovation.ca

Kid Innovation Inc.
www.kidinnovation.com

Have a
2004 World Champion
of Public Speaking
Finalist
speak at your next
event!

In 2004 Rob Nickel competed at the World Championship of Public Speaking in Reno, Nevada.

There were over 30,000 people who had entered and Rob was one of nine finalists to compete at the World Championship Level.

Rob now speaks to parents, teachers, law enforcement and other groups to make them aware of the dangers that lurk online.

Using stories from past investigations, Rob's presentations are educational, entertaining and filled with information that will help keep children safe in a Wired World.

To have Rob speak at your next event you can contact him at:

Rob Nickel
"The Cyber-Safety Expert"
250 Dundas St. South, Unit #6
Cambridge, Ontario.
N1R 8A8

Phone:(519)654-0002
or e-mail
rob@cyber-safety.com
w w w . c y b e r - s a f e t y . c o m